THE ANIMATOR'S WORKBOOK

Copyright © 1986 Tony White

First published in 1986 in New York by Watson-Guptill Publications, a division of Billboard Publications, Inc., 1515 Broadway, New York, N.Y. 10036

Library of Congress Cataloging-in-Publication Data
White, Tony, 1947—
  The animator's workbook.
  Includes index.
  1. Moving-picture cartoons—Technique. I. Title.
NC1765.W48 1986   741.5'8   86-1346
ISBN 0-8230-0228-4

Manufactured in Japan

First printing, 1986
1 2 3 4 5 6 7 8 9 10/91 90 89 88 87 86

To my parents—Dorothy and Richard White—who sacrificed much to get me through art school and subsequently onto my animation path in life, and . . .

To my wife and children—Tricia, Sarah, and Anna—who, sadly, have had to endure many frustrating and neglected hours, seeing only the back of my head, as I have struggled over my unaffectionate and unresponsive lightbox.

ACKNOWLEDGMENTS

This book was conceived, following a series of ten lectures I gave at the Animus Productions studios in London during the winter of 1984–85. The intention was to give students a definitive grounding in the basic principles of animation, based on my invaluable experiences over my many years in the animation world. In response to the encouragement I received during and after the lectures, the idea evolved to develop a book that would present all the information to a wider audience.

Obviously, many influences go into the creation of such a work, and it would be wholly wrong for me to suggest that everything contained within these pages is solely of my own creation. I therefore wish to acknowledge and sincerely thank all the following contributors for the part they have played—great or small—in the production of this book.

☐ To the late, great Ken Harris, for his kind and generous responses to my intensive questioning when working with him for one complete summer.

☐ To the master animator Art Babbit for his wise and learned animation lectures, which brought alive for me the beauty and simplicity of the animator's art.

☐ To many of the "great old men" of animation—particularly Grim Natwick, Abe Levitow, and Frank Thomas, for their encouragement and advice.

☐ To the animation maestro Richard Williams, who is without doubt the singular most important figure in the contemporary animation world today, and without whose influence the British animation scene would undoubtably still be in the condition of ignorance and primitiveness it once knew.

☐ To Carl Gover for his very real support, encouragement, and enthusiasm in producing the majority of my works for many years.

☐ To Larry, Mark, and Ray of Unicorn Projects, Washington, for giving me the opportunity to direct my first TV special—*Cathedral*—and for allowing me the opportunity of reproducing artwork from that production in this book.

☐ And last, but not least, to friend and fellow-director Richard Burdett—and indeed, all of the staff at Animus Productions—for loyal, valued, and constant support since our early, formative days in the studio.

I would also like to thank the firms listed on page 160 for allowing me to use material from the various advertising films I have been involved with over the years, and also Tony Peake, Barbara Miller, Glorya Hale, Sue Heinemann, and Bob Fillie for making this book possible in the first place.

CONTENTS

INTRODUCTION

This is a frame from an animation sequence. If you turn to the back of the book and flip forward, you will see the sequence in animation.

Animation is not just a series of funny drawings strung together in movement. At its most creative, it is a truly beautiful art form. Yet the tradition of drawn animation is a relatively short one compared with other visual arts. It has only been in this century that the technology to produce any film—let alone an animated film—has been available. Indeed, I have often thought that many of the Old Masters, from Leonardo da Vinci to Rembrandt to Hokusai, might well have committed themselves to animation, had the knowledge of filmmaking been available to them in their time.

Animated filmmaking, in its widest expression, is not, however, traditionally an art form of individual genius. A large team of dedicated, talented, and cooperative artists is required to complete a high-quality animation film. Successful animation demands a collective creative approach, within which each individual, no matter how talented, must harmonize and communicate with others for his or her work to be given its fullest expression on the screen. Problems can arise when the methods and terminology used by any one individual on the team are not compatible or familiar to the others. Although it is impossible to demand that all individual creative artists work in an identical manner one objective of this workbook is to offer a standard terminology and method of approach for all beginning animators as well as existing practitioners to work with confidently.

Admittedly, no one person can have a perfect understanding of animation. As in life, the animation artist may come to view only one or two facets of the greater whole. Style, taste, content, and objectives are many and varied, and this book cannot and does not provide all the answers. It is a guide to the accepted, traditional animation techniques devised over many years, and strives to be no more than that.

At its best, animation is a wonderfully varied art form, which potentially has no limitations on imagination or technique. Sadly, exciting ideas are often spoiled by inadequate animation ability and fall into a pit of undisciplined sloppiness. In addition to being an art, animation is a craft and, as with any craft, it takes time for apprentices to master it. The rudiments of the craft, however, can be taught relatively quickly. What is then needed is patience, commitment, and effort, to make the basic principles come alive with new life and fresh ideas. In the early days of animation, Walt Disney established a fine tradition of craftsmanship, which we can only look up to, from our more humble position of expertise. What has been achieved once, however, can theoretically be achieved again if the will, the financial support, and the working knowledge are there.

This workbook is designed to give you the necessary basic knowledge to start on the path toward becoming an animator. But it is only your commitment and effort that will prove, in the long run, whether or not you are capable of becoming a great one. To be a great animator is to lead a life of concentration, observation, dedication, and inspiration—as well as many long hours of perspiration. It is not an easy life, and often it is only when the work is up there on the screen that it suddenly, somehow, all seems worth it.

THE PROCESS OF ANIMATION

The first step in learning about animation is to understand the procedures involved in making an animated film.

Animation, at best, is a costly procedure, in both time and money, and anything that eases its birth process should not be ignored. If audiences only knew all that is involved in any animated production, their respect for what I consider one of the most creative art forms would increase.

On a large-scale production, it is important that the team function efficiently. A typical team for the production of a large-scale animated film includes a lot of people: a director; a producer; a number of animators and assistant animators; possibly a team of inbetweeners; a whole assortment of cleanup artists, tracers, painters and renderers, and special-effects artists; plus several checkers, editors, and rostrum cameramen. In addition, there is the production and administrative staff. Considering all the personalities involved, it is often a miracle that any animation films get made at all.

Whether the film being produced is a 30-second television commercial or a full-length animated feature, the process of animation should follow certain structured procedures. If these procedures are adhered to at the outset, then all will be well. But failing to respect these guidelines can prove extremely costly in time and money, regardless of the individual skills of the personnel involved.

Script. The first stage of any film production is the creation of the script, and, as for any other production, the script for an animation film is extremely important. This film script differs, however, from the live-action film script. With live action, dialogue is of great importance to the actor's performance. With the animation film script, on the other hand, dialogue is less important, and, indeed, complicated dialogue should be avoided as much as possible. It is the visual action in plot and performance that is paramount. The best animation is achieved through a form of mimed action, where dialogue is nonexistent and the visual invention captures the imagination.

After the storyboard is completed, members of the team discuss various aspects of character design.

Storyboard. From the script, the director produces a storyboard, a series of drawn images that graphically portray the action described in the script. Often, while producing the storyboard, deficiencies in the structure and format of the script are detected and corrected by the director. The storyboard, then, allows the writer, director, producer, and animation team to see and appreciate the content of the project. If the project is more ambitious than a 30-second television commercial, often a think tank, comprised of all the contributors involved, is set up and the story, content, and ideas are finely polished.

Soundtrack. After the script and storyboard are completed, the recording of any dialogue or key music is undertaken. Since animation relies totally on perfect synchronization of the picture to the soundtrack, the animator must receive the final recorded track before beginning to draw. Without it, the animator cannot time the action accurately. When the action is in sync with music, it should be possible to record a simple guide track, with a minimum of musicians, to indicate the essential beat and the basic melodies. A click track—which has a predetermined click, or beat, overlaid onto it—serves this purpose.

Track Breakdown. When the soundtrack has been made, an editor assembles it into the precise working length of the film and then breaks down the track. Basically, the breakdown is a simple process of analyzing the dialogue phonetically—by sound rather than by spelling—and documenting the precise position of each sound in relation to the film frames. If, for instance, a character begins to cough after one second of film time (35mm movie film is projected at 24 frames per second), the editor marks the beginning of the cough on the 25th frame and then indicates the subsequent frames through which the cough continues. The entire track breakdown is transferred to the bar sheet, a preprinted sheet designed to allow every frame of soundtrack and film to be identified and analyzed visually (see page 132).

Designs. While the soundtrack is being broken down, the director selects one or more film designers to produce visual interpretations of all the characters featured in the film. When these interpretations are approved, each character is drawn from a multitude of angles and placed on a single sheet of paper, called a model sheet, for all the animators to use as a reference. In addition to the character designs, at this stage, ideally, the background styling for all the principal sequences in the film is produced.

Leica Reel. Using the bar sheets and storyboard, the layout artist (under the supervision of the director) proceeds to produce a Leica reel of the whole film. A Leica reel is, in essence, a filmed storyboard, which can be projected in synchronization with the final soundtrack. Rather than filming the storyboard drawings (which are often merely scribbles), the layout artist carefully draws each scene to the size at which it will eventually be animated. In addition, the layout artist draws the characterization in the precise style created by the film designer and describes, perhaps in more than one drawing, the action in that scene. When all the scenes of the film have been completed in this way, the director—using the bar sheet to obtain the

Wearing white cotton gloves helps to prevent smudges in the drawings.

Color is painted on the back of the cel drawing.

relevant timings—has each scene shot on film. The director then views the finished Leica reel to get an impression of the way the film is shaping up. At this point the director can, of course, still make changes in the visual content of the film, before any of the costly animation work is undertaken. Indeed, the Leica-reel viewing is often the last chance the director has to change the film without affecting time and money costs on what is normally a tight schedule and budget.

Line Tests. When the Leica reel is acceptable to the director and producer, the animators finally become involved in the film and begin to produce a line test of each scene. Line tests are the animation drawings, produced in pencil on paper, filmed to the precise timings of the scene, as indicated on the bar sheet. Sometimes it is necessary to alter the animation several times in a particular scene, if the line test shows that the action is not quite working. Usually, however, the line test works the first time and the scene can be cut into the Leica reel by the editor, thus replacing the drawings originally produced by the layout artist. Gradually, as each pencil-animated scene is added, a line test of the whole film becomes available for viewing and for fine adjustment. Any major changes from this stage onward may prove extremely damaging to the overall film budget.

Cleanup. On a major production it is ideal to have a team of cleanup artists on staff. They take all the animation drawings and clean them up, to give them a consistent visual style. This is important because, when many animators are working on the same character, there is an inevitable variation in the look of the character. After the entire cleanup is completed, it is best to line-test the drawings again, just to check that no additional mistakes have slipped in.

Trace and Paint. When a cleaned-up line test is finally approved, each drawing is transferred to a thin sheet of celluloid or acetate—a cel—and painted in the colors of the original design. In the early days of animation, transferring the drawings to cels involved large teams of trained artists, who carefully traced each drawing required in a varied range of line techniques.

Today, however, it is possible to quickly photocopy a drawing on the cel or for the cleanup artists and animators to draw directly on the cel itself, avoiding the pencil stage altogether. After the animated image is on cel, and in preparation for the final shoot, a team of artists paints the cel in opaque colors on the reverse side to the drawing, thus keeping the paint from going over the lines and producing flatter, smoother colors.

Backgrounds. While the animation is being traced and painted, another team of artists produces the backgrounds—everything behind or, sometimes, in front of the moving characters that does not move. Each background artist must achieve a continuity of style by producing work identical to the original film design style.

Checking. As the finished animation cels and backgrounds are completed scene by scene, they are passed to the checker, who makes sure that everything is correctly drawn, traced, painted, and prepared for the cameraman who is to finally film it. It is essential that the checker be efficient; incomplete or incorrect work discovered during the final shoot results in wasted time and money.

Final Shoot. When the checker is satisfied that all the artwork for each scene is right, the artwork is passed on to the rostrum camerman, who shoots the completed scene. As its name implies, the final shoot is the final stage in the actual filming procedure related to the artwork.

Rushes. After the final shoot is completed, the exposed film is sent to the film laboratories for overnight processing. It returns the following morning, ready for projection as rushes. The rushes are viewed for possible errors. If any are found, the problem must be identified and rectified, and the scene reshot. If, on the other hand, everything is fine, the rushes are cut by the editor into the final film, replacing the existing line-test scenes.

Dubbing. When the whole film exists in final form, and the director is satisfied with it, the editor, with the director, proceeds to choose sound effects (SFX) to go with the action in the film. After all the sound effects are chosen and laid in perfect synchronization with the action, the editor and director go into a dubbing theater, where the voice track, music, and sound effects are all mixed on one complete soundtrack. This leaves the film in a completed double-head stage—with the finished picture and the finished soundtrack on two separate rolls of film.

Answer Print. From the double-head, the editor orders an answer print from the film laboratories. This involves merging the sound and picture on one piece of film—after an extensive session of picture grading (checking, scene by scene, that the colors of the picture are accurately reproduced). The sound aspect of an answer print, called an optical track, entails the transfer of all the sound elements of the film to a varying-intensity visual format. There is now a thin, visual strip along one side of the film and, when light is projected through it, the variations in light intensity are converted by the sound system to variations in sound intensity.

Finally, the completed answer print is projected and receives—everyone hopes—a spontaneous round of enthusiastic applause.

THE ANIMATOR'S TOOLKIT

Animation is an exacting art, so it is important to have the appropriate tools for its creation.

In addition to the obvious pencils and erasers, there is a whole range of items that, ideally, the animator needs access to when working on a film. The following list has been compiled with a large production in mind and may seem prohibitively expensive to most students and amateur film-makers. It must therefore be stressed that animation can be produced with a minimum of equipment and facilities.

Paper and Cel. There is no specific paper on which animation should be drawn, although the paper must be substantial enough to flip (that is, for you to hold a whole series of sheets of animation drawings together in one hand and flip them with the other hand to simulate the moving action and check it for obvious flaws). At the same time, the paper must be translucent enough for you to see the essentials of the next drawing through the top sheet. Whatever paper is used, it must first be punched for registration pegs and almost always cut to the standard 12-inch or 15-inch field sizes (described on page 90). Animation supply companies provide ready-punched and ready-cut paper and cel on request.

Acetate, or cel, for animation can be bought in various degrees of thickness. If it is too thick, however, it will not allow sufficient light through for you to see any artwork placed below it when several levels are shot together. The standard thickness for animation cel is 0.090 mm (0.005 inch) with a range from 0.075 mm to 0.125 mm.

Paper and Cel Punch. All animation is registered by placing each punched sheet of paper or cel consecutively on standardized registration pegs, so it does not move in relation to the other sheets. If you do not use ready-punched animation paper and cel, then you will need a peg-hole punch for registration. For the professional, two regular systems are available; each basically consists of one round hole in the center of the animation paper or cel, with a long hole to either side of it, to avoid any pivoting of the paper.

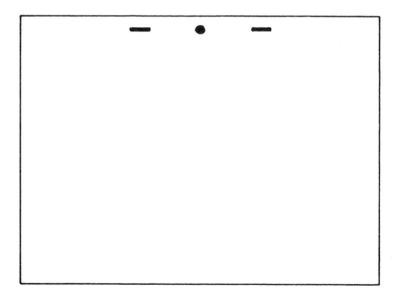

For the beginner and amateur filmmaker, however, it is possible to construct a system using an ordinary office hole punch, available from office supply stores.

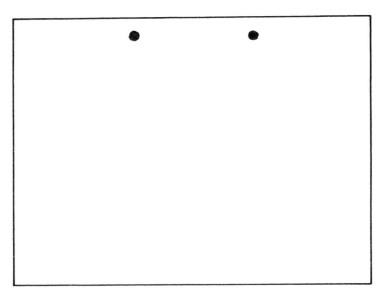

Peg Bar. Obviously, if the animation paper or cel is punched for registration, it must be suitable for the registration system used. This registration system involves placing the paper on a peg bar, which can be purchased from any animation supplier or good art store. Before you buy the peg bar, however, make sure that its peg system is compatible with the peg system of your punch, or the ready-punched paper and cel available to you.

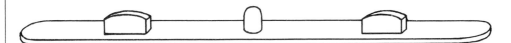

The nonprofessional can easily construct a peg bar by inserting two thin wooden dowels in the work surface and making sure they are positioned in perfect alignment with the punch holes produced by the office hole punch.

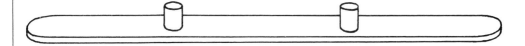

The peg bar can be positioned at the top of the animation paper (top pegs) or at the bottom (bottom pegs). There is no one correct position, and all animators have their own preferences. In my opinion, however, it is usually better to use top pegs, because bottom pegs tend to get in the way of the animator's hand while drawing. The only time I would use bottom pegs is when the animation is near the top of the screen, so top pegs would tend to be a handicap while drawing.

Lightbox. Most animation work is concerned with slight changes of movement from drawing to drawing. It is therefore necessary to see two or more drawings in relation to each other at the same time. Because this is best achieved by illuminating the surface beneath the paper, it is recommended that the animator use a lightbox. A simple lightbox has an adjustable frame, which supports an ample work surface and can be angled for drawing comfort. Set into the frame is a sheet of white translucent plastic. Beneath the plastic (and far enough away to avoid the plastic being melted), there is a fluorescent tube, which, when switched on, allows light to shine through the white plastic. A peg bar is then taped to the top of the plastic, in a suitable position, and the paper or cel can be placed on top.

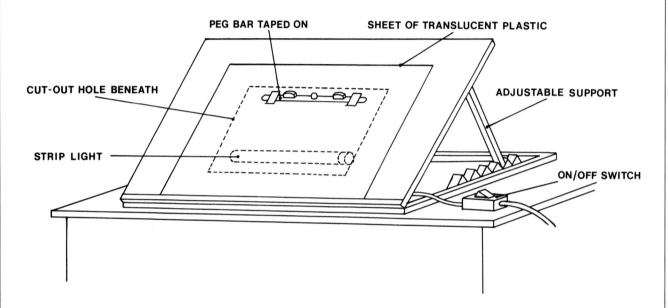

A more sophisticated arrangement involves a circular sheet of white plastic set into a cast-metal, circular frame, with round finger holes cut into the top and bottom for easy turning. This movable disk can be used to turn the drawing for easier execution of the drawing line. Some professional lightboxes also have movable top and bottom peg bars, with fine increment markings for calculating artwork that is to be panned.

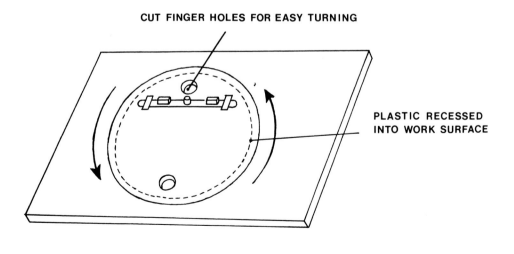

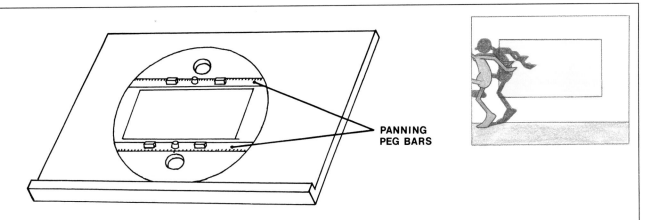

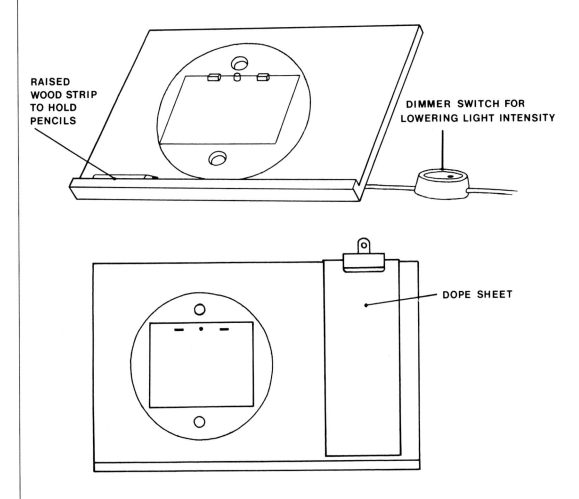

Additional refinements to the lightbox might include a raised strip of wood along the bottom of the frame for holding pencils and a dimmer switch (instead of the on/off switch) so that the intensity of light coming through can be varied. If you are constructing your own lightbox, it is advantageous to leave sufficient space to the right of the disk (if you are right-handed) or to the left (if you are left-handed) so there is room to place the camera instruction, or dope sheets, for easy reference.

Electric Pencil Sharpener. Although it may seem a luxury to the uninitiated, anyone working in full-time animation is likely to purchase an electric pencil sharpener. Such an aid is invaluable when a great deal of drawing has to be done and time is of essence. In other circumstances, of course, a manual pencil sharpener is sufficient.

Peg Reinforcements. Often, when animation drawings are shot over and over again, the peg holes on each drawing become worn or damaged. To avoid this, it is useful to have a supply of peg reinforcements, which, when stuck over the peg holes, protect them from unnecessary damage. These are readily available from any animation supply store.

Graticule. One essential item that the animator should have available is a field-size graticule, which, when placed on the pegs, provides a reference guide to the area of the drawing that the camera will pick up. The area chosen for the camera to cover in any piece of art is known as the field size. There are traditionally two standard field sizes for animation—12 inches and 15 inches—and suitable graticules for both are readily available (see page 90).

Bar Sheets and Dope Sheets. Normally, the animator does not have to provide the editor with blank bar sheets because these are standard equipment in the editing room. The animator is, however, expected to have a supply of dope sheets, which are used for the camera instructions. The soundtrack information has to be transferred from the bar sheets to the dope sheets before the commencement of animation, so animators are well advised to check that their dope sheet grid is compatible with the grid on the editor's bar sheet. For nonprofessional use, however, a simple dope sheet arrangement can be drawn up and photocopied, according to needs. (See page 88, for an example of a typical dope sheet format.)

Production Folders. In large-scale studio productions, it is essential that the dope sheet instructions for each scene be kept separate from each other, to avoid the catastrophe of all this information being muddled up. For these productions, all the dope sheet information is stapled into a cardboard folder, known as a production folder. On the outside of each production folder, a great deal of information can be written, including the production title, sequence number, scene number, scene title, footage length, animator's name, and assistant animator's name, as well as such stages in production as backgrounds, trace and paint, effects animation, and checking. After the work on a particular stage is completed, it can be initialed by a representative of the department concerned. In this way, if any problem crops up

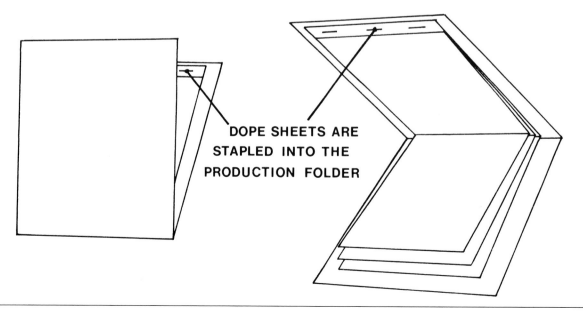

DOPE SHEETS ARE STAPLED INTO THE PRODUCTION FOLDER

relating to a particular scene, it is immediately possible to identify the person who worked on that aspect of the scene, and who, therefore, is most likely to have the solution to the problem.

All the artwork for each scene, as well as all the information relating to that scene, should be kept with the production folder at all times. Failure to do this can cause a great deal of trouble—particularly on a large production, which has to run smoothly and economically. On a small production, however, a production folder is not absolutely necessary if the animator is reasonably well organized.

Paper/Cel Rack. Another organizing tool for the animator is a paper/cel rack. This is merely a unit of closely ranged shelves, which can hold in a small space a selection of animation paper and cel, production folders, scenes to animate, scenes that have been animated, and visual reference material. An average paper/cel rack measures 20 inches (50.8 cm) wide and 20 inches deep and stands about 30 inches (76.2 cm) high. The shelves should be placed at approximately three-inch intervals.

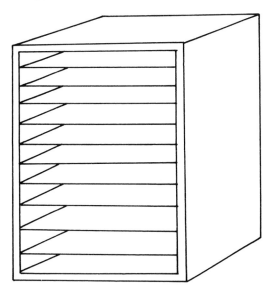

Mirror. When tackling dialogue, the animator needs a mirror to refer to. By miming the animated dialogue, in front of a mirror, the animator gains insight into the mechanics of the actual mouth movements involved.

Cassette Player. When animating to dialogue or to a music track, the animator must be able to play the soundtrack over and over again, to identify the main emphasis points. It is best to have the soundtrack transferred to a cassette tape to be replayed at leisure on a cassette player.

Movie or Video Camera. Finally, when all the pencil drawings are done, it is essential to test the full animation, to check its movement. In professional studios, rostrum camera facilities are readily available, but, for the student or amateur, it is necessary to obtain a stop-frame super-8 or 16 mm camera, as well as the means to project the film when processed. If you are serious about doing animation work, however, it is recommended that you invest in a single-frame video camera unit. With this unit, the animation drawings can be shot and reviewed instantly, thereby saving time and avoiding the need to use outside camera facilities and laboratories. Of course, the final shoot must be done on film.

INBETWEENING

Inbetweening—producing the drawings inbetween the key drawings—is of fundamental importance to the success or failure of animation technique.

An inbetween is a drawing that is usually exactly between two extremes, or key drawings. Consider for example, a ball rolling from A to C.

The inbetween of A to C is (B):

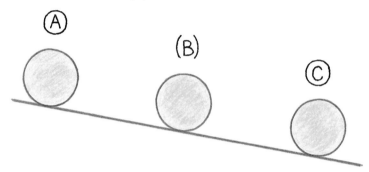

If the animator wants more inbetweens between the key drawings (say, 1 to 9), they would appear as:

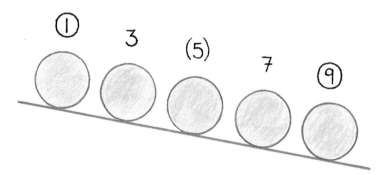

In a studio, inbetweening is done by the assistant. It is essential that the assistant accurately carry out what the animator has indicated, even when inbetweening under pressure. Bad inbetweening can turn a potentially excellent piece of smooth animation into a staccato movement, irritating to the eye. Sloppy inbetweening has to be redone, costing the studio money, threatening the production schedule, and creating additional work for two people, who should be moving on to other things. Obviously, the fundamental requirement of inbetweening is accuracy.

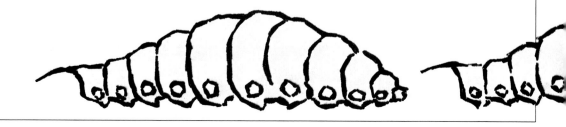

Charts and Breakdown Drawings

To tell the assistant just how many inbetweens are needed between two keys, the animator draws a chart on the first key (drawing 1).

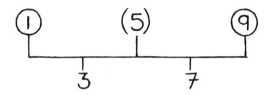

Drawing (5) is indicated in parentheses because it is the first inbetween to be done between 1 and 9 (the key drawings, which are circled). It is called the breakdown drawing.

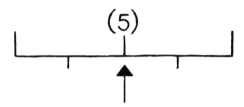

When the breakdown is completed, the assistant must put in the two in-between drawings: drawing 3 in the middle of 1 and (5), and drawing 7 in the middle of (5) and 9.

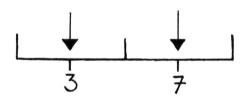

When all the inbetween drawings are completed, each is shot separately in sequence on a rostrum camera (usually two frames of film for each draw-ing, although for more sophisticated work it is often necessary to do one drawing per frame). There can be any number of equal inbetweens between two key drawings, but usually the animator does not leave the assistant more than three consecutive inbetweens at any one time. Often the ani-mator draws the breakdown drawing to help the assistant.

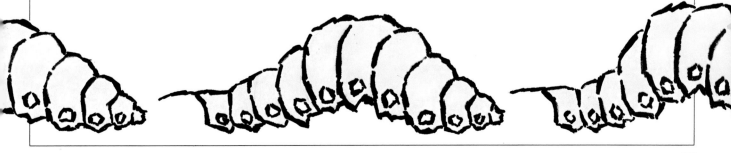

Sometimes, the animator wants the movement to slow down or to speed up between two key drawings. In this case, the key chart is drawn differently. Always remember that the more drawings used to produce a movement, the slower the movement will be. Conversely, the fewer drawings within a movement, the faster it will be. Therefore, if the animator places more in-betweens at the end of a movement, it will appear to slow down when filmed. The chart would look like this:

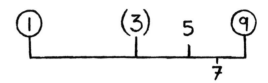

This setup is known as a slow-in, because the action is slowing in to the final key position. (Note that the breakdown drawing is number 3 in this chart.) If, on the other hand, the animator places most of the inbetweens at the beginning of the movement, and wants the action to speed up as it moves, this is known as slowing out. (Note that on the chart the breakdown drawing is now number 7.)

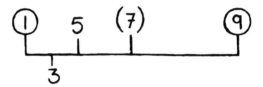

Sometimes, in a longer movement, the animator may want the action to speed up, then slow down, between two key positions. This is known as a slowing-out and slowing-in movement. In this situation, to help the assistant, the animator would probably draw the breakdown drawing, as well as the two key drawings.

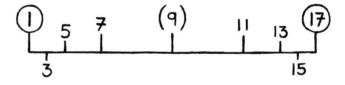

Remember that the key drawings are always circled, and the breakdown drawing is always in parentheses.

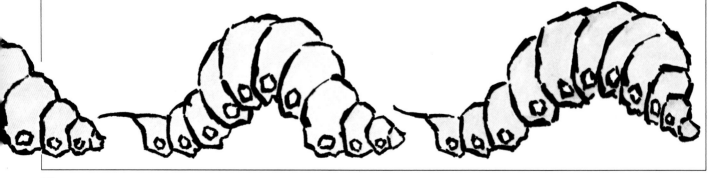

Sometimes an animator wants an even movement between two key drawings, but can use only two inbetweens to accomplish this because the soundtrack limits the time for the action. In this case, the animator charts the two inbetweens on thirds—that is, each is positioned one-third of the way between two keys.

Thirds are rarely used, however. It is often just as easy to use either a slow-in or a slow-out.

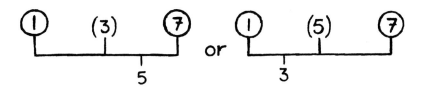

Nevertheless, if a third is unavoidable, it is unfair for the animator to leave the assistant to position it, unless it is extremely simple. The animator should always draw in one of the thirds before passing it on for inbetweening. This saves a lot of time (and hair tearing) for the assistant. If the animator does not indicate one of the thirds, it is reasonable for the assistant to ask the animator for guidance on this initial placement.

Obviously, animators do not always draw dots moving, and a great deal of change in shape and form may take place between two key drawings. For example, one shape (1) may turn into another (9) in even inbetweens.

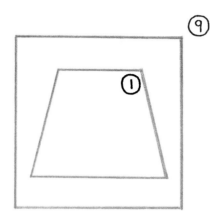

The chart will then read:

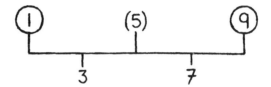

In this example, the assistant has to use visual judgment to find a series of key points that link the important midpoints between the two shapes. The assistant lightly marks these points (usually in blue pencil) before making the final breakdown drawing. Having accurately plotted the key points, the assistant then links the key points in a smooth, natural line, which constitutes the finished breakdown drawing. After the breakdown drawing is completed, the inbetweens are achieved in an identical way—with 3 drawn between 1 and (5), and 7 drawn between (5) and 9.

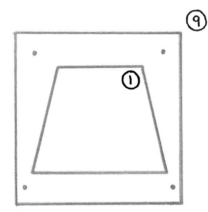 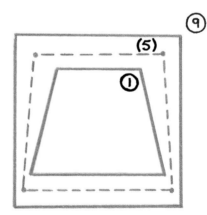 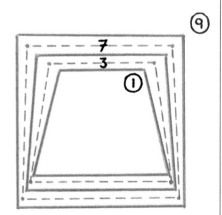

If the shape is changing, it is almost always necessary for the position of one key to be different from the position of the next key. The first shape might be in one part of the screen and the transformed shape in another area.

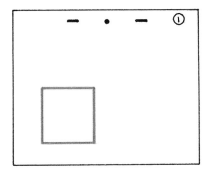 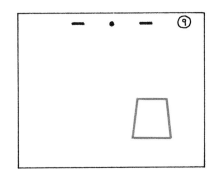

In this situation, even greater visual judgment must be exercised by the assistant. First, the center points of the two shapes must be lightly drawn in blue; then the center key point of the breakdown drawing is marked on its separate sheet of paper.

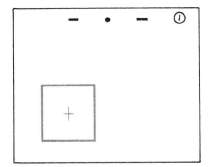 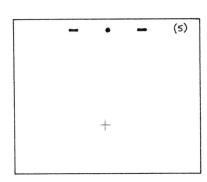 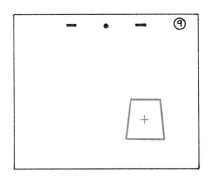

The assistant then removes the breakdown drawing and the top key drawing from the pegs. The top key is superimposed over the bottom key so that the shapes' centers align, one above the other. The top key is then lightly taped down with camera tape, away from the drawing area. Next, the breakdown sheet is superimposed over the two key drawings (again, center above center) and taped down.

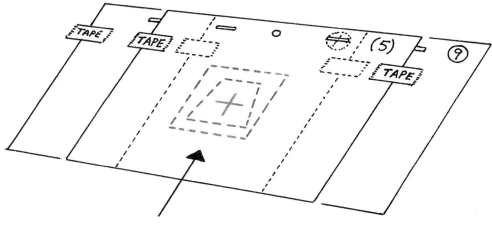

CENTERS ALIGNED

When doing this, the assistant must make sure that all three sheets remain perfectly square to one another. If one sheet twists in any direction, there will be a twist in the final breakdown drawing—making it inaccurate.

After all three sheets have been secured, the breakdown drawing is completed. The sheets are then untaped and replaced on the registration pegs, and a quick visual check is made for any possible error. The breakdown drawing should now be perfectly placed; the inbetweens can then be calculated and drawn, using the same procedures.

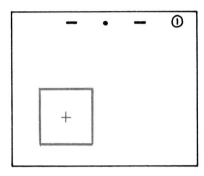
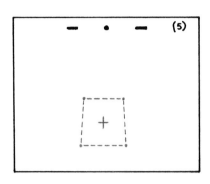
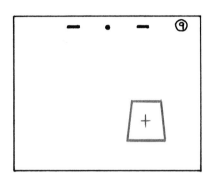

Often, however, it is not possible to use the center as a point of reference when marking the key points between two key drawings. In this case, the assistant must again use visual judgment to estimate the approximate positions of the moving form and mass, and mark them lightly in blue in the relevant inbetween positions on the breakdown sheet. Obviously, if there are similar points of design in the two key drawings, the assistant is greatly aided in assessing the key points. If, for example, a cube is moving into a pyramid, the base will have common key points—the corners—but the top will not. Marking the key points for the base is therefore easy, but the assistant must assess the rest. A lightly drawn breakdown assessment might appear as:

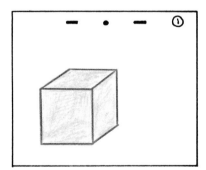
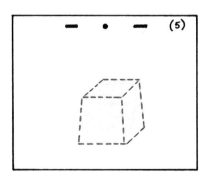
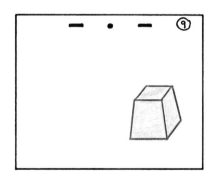

Having made this assessment, the assistant superimposes the drawings (key points over key points). The breakdown drawing can then be completed more accurately, eliminating potential visual errors.

Arcs

It is often necessary for the animator to make the action move along an arc, or curved path of action. This makes it much more difficult for the assistant, whose visualizing capacity is stretched even further. Consider a pendulum that is swinging from one side of the screen to the other:

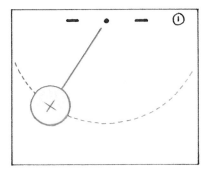 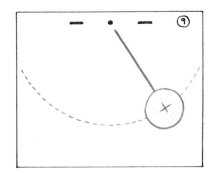

The breakdown drawing would be assessed as:

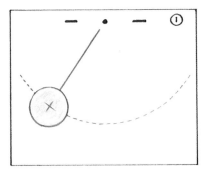 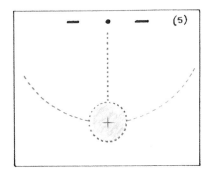 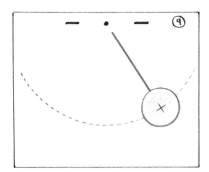

To do the breakdown drawing, the assistant must remember that the pendulum is swinging on an arc. This time, for the superimposition, the sheets of paper must be placed out-of-square (using the arm and the center of the pendulum circle as the key points for aligning the drawings). The final breakdown drawing can be completed as before, and—if it is correct—the inbetweens can be done in the same way.

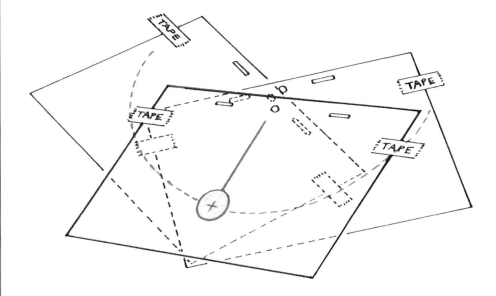

33

It is always irritating to see parts of the animation suddenly freeze, while other parts of the scene are freely animated. This sudden freeze occurs when a held drawing is used. It is preferable (although more expensive from a budgetary point of view) for the assistant to trace back the stationary parts of the breakdown, or inbetween, from one or the other of the two keys in question. Basically this means that the assistant must precisely trace, on all the inbetweens, the parts of the action that are not moving. Although these nonmoving parts could be placed on a held cel for economy, when filmed the traceback drawings have life, which the held drawing does not.

To work perfectly, the tracebacks must be extremely accurate. When doing tracebacks, the drawing to be traced should be taped down at the edge opposite the registration pegs. This eliminates inaccurate tracing due to slippage of the paper caused by the movements of the drawing hand.

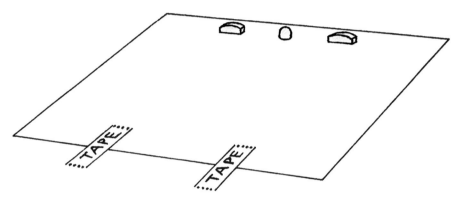

The golden rule of tracebacks is that they should always be traced from the original key, indicated by the animator, and never from any of the inbetween drawings subsequently produced. Failure to follow this rule always results in inaccuracies.

Assignment

Copy the two key drawings shown here and inbetween each action as indicated by the chart instructions. Then film each drawing on twos (two frames per drawing). Shoot the drawings consecutively, 1 to 9, then back from 9 to 1, without a break. Repeat this six times without interruption. When viewing your tests, try to run them over and over again on a loop. Look for jumps, kicks, or any other inaccuracies that disrupt the smooth movement of the action.

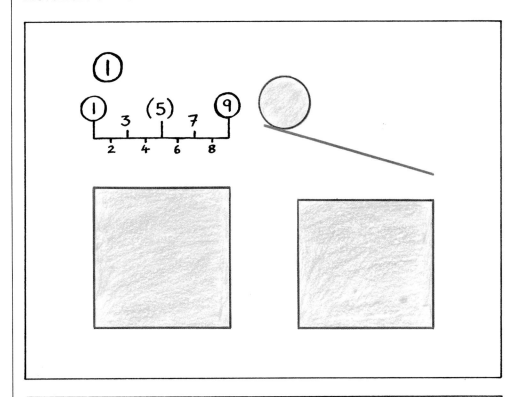

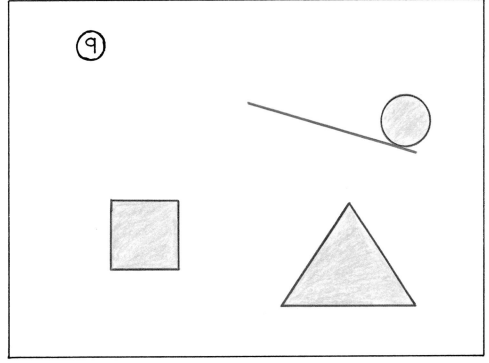

HEAD TURNS

Producing realistic head turns requires careful inbetweening.

Remember that everything that moves in life, moves in arcs. This is true of everything but a machine, which, by its very nature, is mechanical. The animator must always bear this in mind when animating and the assistant must also bear it in mind when attempting a breakdown. Consider these two key drawings, which show a head turning from front to profile (1 to 9).

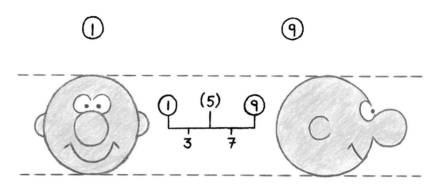

How is the breakdown drawing drawn? The way that it is not drawn is as a straight inbetween:

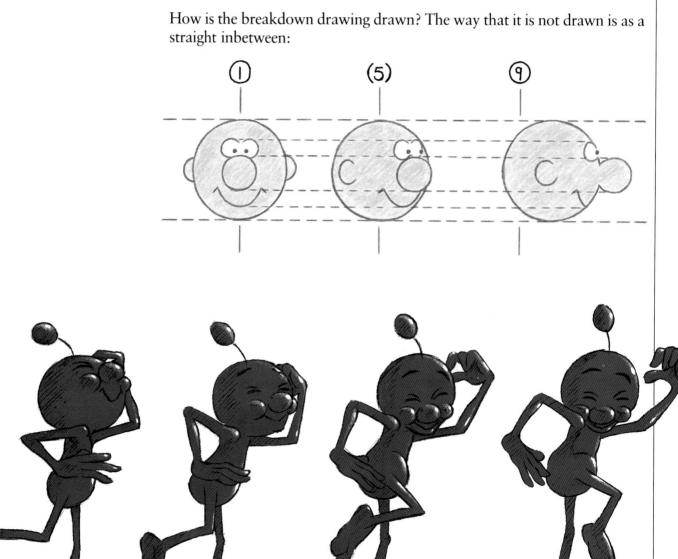

A straight inbetween will cause the features of the face to slide across the head and make the action look mechanical. To avoid this and make the action appear more realistic, the breakdown must be placed on an arc. If you turn your own head and feel what is happening, you will be conscious of a slight dip in its path of action as it turns. This is the arc that has to be imitated in the animation. A more natural breakdown thus appears as:

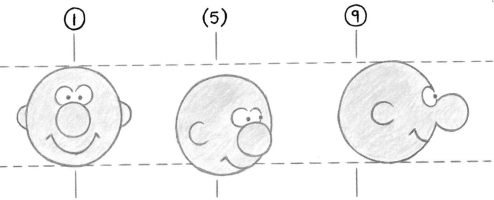

Additional inbetweens follow the same arc:

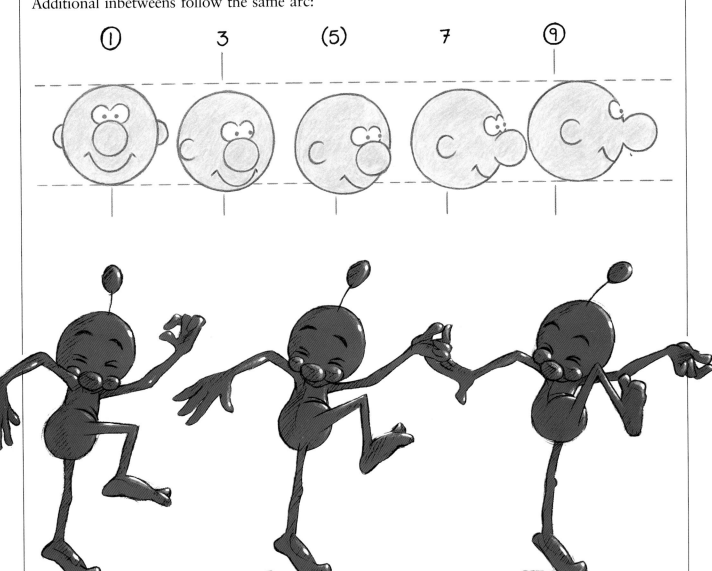

When animating, it is essential that you feel the character's movements in your own body before you begin to move the character—very much as actors must feel their way into a part before playing the role. The greater your imagination, the greater your potential for producing convincing animation.

If you turn your own head rapidly to the side, you may become aware that your eyes either blink fully or half-close as your head turns. In other words, your own personal breakdown position has an eye change, which you can integrate into your animated head movement by closing the eyes on breakdown (5).

(5)

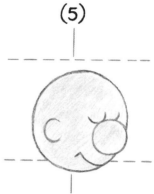

A few additional tips concerning eyes may be helpful here. If, for example, the pupil is moving from one side of the eye to the other, it is also essential that the action move on an arc—otherwise, a sliding effect will occur. The movement of the pupil should be:

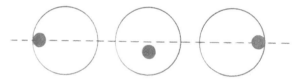

If the pupil is moving on one side of the eyeball, up or down, then it becomes more convincing if the circle of the eyeball is stretched slightly where the pupil touches it.

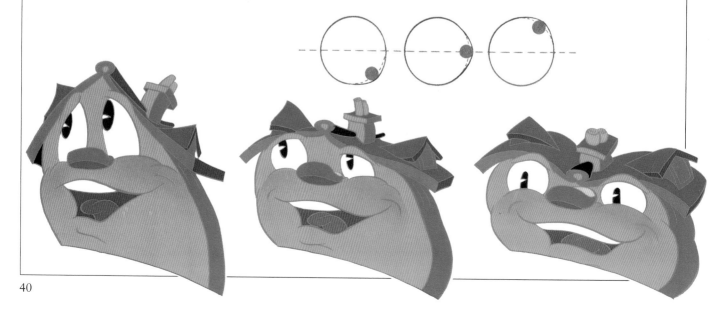

When the character is moving and looking in one direction, the eyes should lead the direction of the head as early in the action as possible.

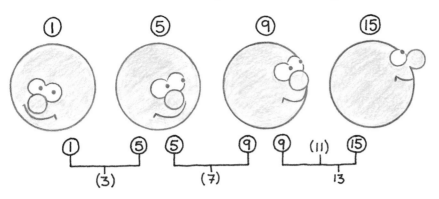

Keep in mind that if the pupil in the eye is very small (A), it gives a dazed, weak, unconvincing look to the character's expression. On the other hand, if the pupil is very large (B), it gives the impression of receptivity and interest.

(A)   (B)

If the pupil touches the rim of the eyeball, it appears forceful (A). But if it is surrounded by white, it looks somewhat vague (B).

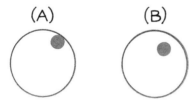

(A)   (B)

When an eye blinks, never draw a straight line in midposition for the breakdown. Either make it curve upward just above the center line, or make it curve downward just below.

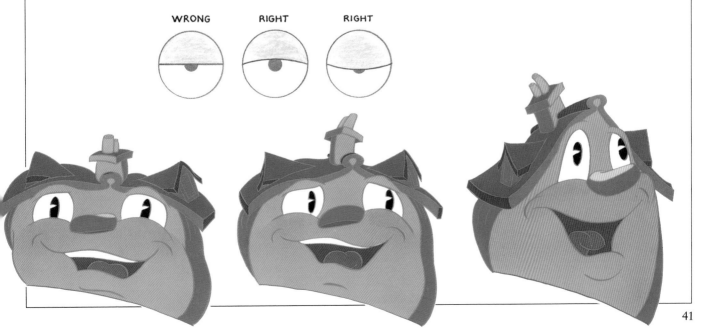

WRONG   RIGHT   RIGHT

The fewer inbetweens from an open to a closed position, and a closed to an open position, the more alert and intelligent the character will seem. The more inbetweens used, the sleepier, or stupider, the character will look. This is an alert blink:

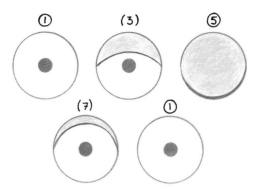

And this is a sleepy blink:

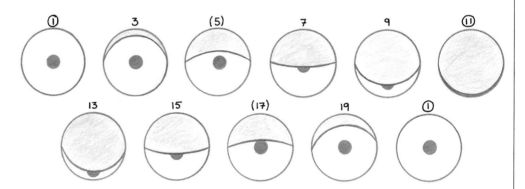

When an eyelid moves on a sleepy blink, it often works best if the pupil is carried down with the eyelid:

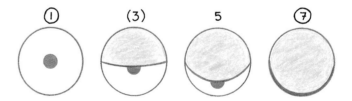

And rises up with the lid when the eye is opening.

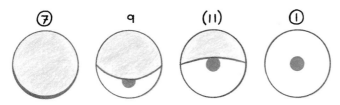

Squints of disbelief are drawn with the bottom and top lids meeting in the middle.

Assignment

First copy the keys provided. Then inbetween the head turning from 1 to 9 on a downward arc, and then from 9 back to 1 on an upward arc. To make this assignment more interesting, place a blink on drawings 1 to 9.

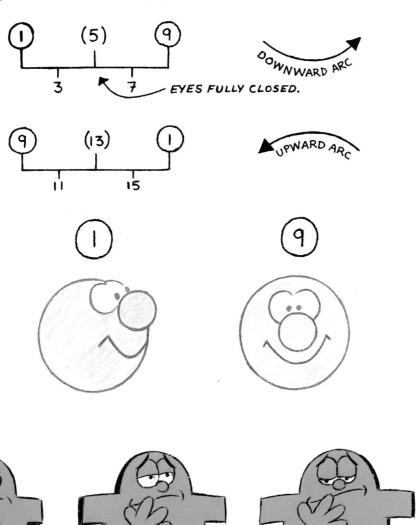

DOWNWARD ARC

EYES FULLY CLOSED.

UPWARD ARC

WALKS

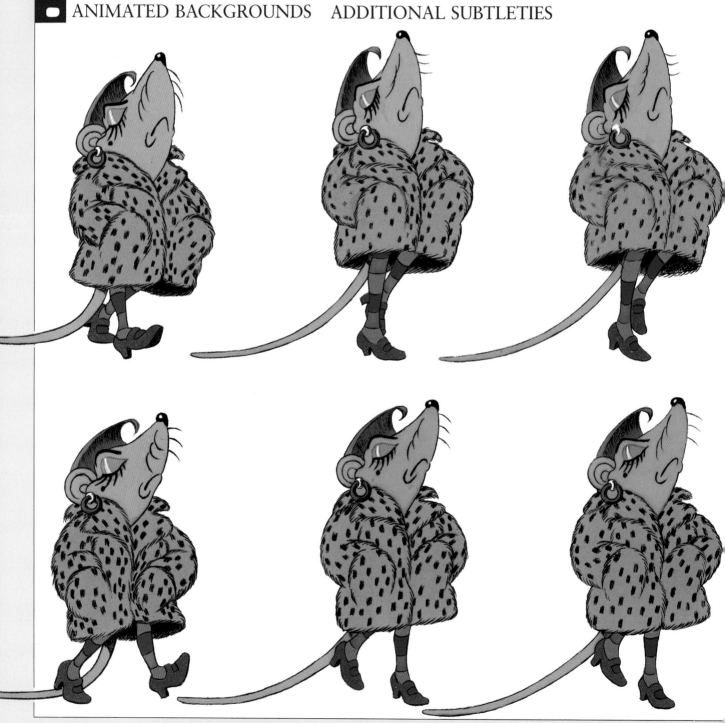

onvincing walks are the most difficult aspect of animation to achieve, but once the art of animating a walk is mastered, it is never forgotten.

Basically, animating a walk merely requires producing two extremes, or key positions, and inbetweening them in a logical way. Unfortunately, however, the human body is a complex piece of machinery and does not lend itself easily to simple procedures. The head, arms, body, and legs all seem to move independently so that it appears impossible to "get into" the action. If, however, you break down the action into sections, the task becomes far simpler.

The main action in a walk stems from the legs and the lower body so we will begin by concentrating on these parts. Basically, a walk is a continuous series of steps. One step looks like this:

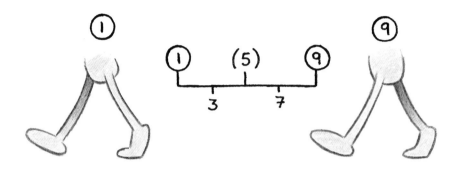

To make the right foot move forward from drawing 1 to drawing 9 (which is one step), we will use three inbetweens. Before you draw any action, however, act it out yourself. Take a step in front of a mirror and observe how it looks and feels when the right foot lifts up from the ground, moves through, and makes contact with the ground in front of you.

For a slow walk, the changes are very subtle from one drawing to the next.

46

The Passing Position

The midway position (5) between any two keys is normally known as the breakdown position, but with walks, it is called the passing position. The passing position between the two step keys (1 and 9) basically looks like this:

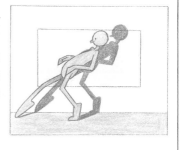

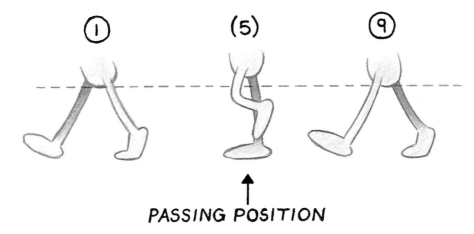

PASSING POSITION

Note, first, that in all walk drawings (with the possible exception of a character who is out of balance, such as a drunk), the body weight is always in balance with the leg positions. More important, the body is raised higher in the passing position than in the key extremes. This is because, in the passing position, the leg is straight beneath the body, and, since the leg does not shrink, it naturally forces the body upward.

Now that the passing position is complete, the inbetween must be put in.

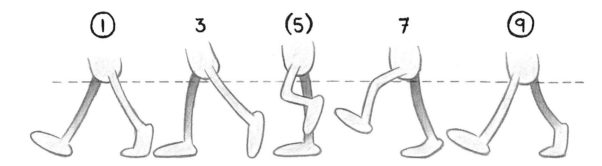

Note that the height of the two inbetween body positions falls naturally between the extremes and the passing position. The free leg, however, is not a natural inbetween. In drawing 3, the toe is still in contact with the ground; otherwise, the body weight would not be in balance with the legs and the figure would seem to fall backward. In drawing 7, the heel of the foot is also touching (or in near contact with) the ground—again, to aid with balance.

This, then, is a standard walk step. To complete the movement, the next step must be animated—from drawing 9 to extreme drawing 17. This time the other foot is the one being lifted up, brought through, and put down ahead of the body.

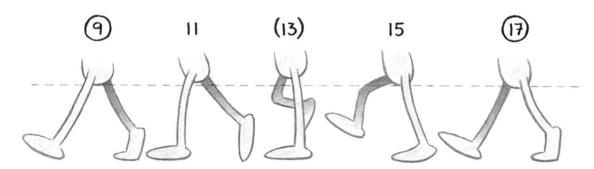

A completed walk, then, looks like this:

Note how the contact foot always locks into the same place on the ground while everything else moves forward. Although this procedure is the most time-consuming way to produce a walk, it does give you the advantage of varying each step, according to the demands of the scene.

Walk Cycles

A much easier way to effect a walk, without producing hundreds of animation drawings, is to use a walk cycle. With a walk cycle, the character's walk is repeated on-the-spot, while the background pans through the scene. A walk cycle is slightly more demanding technically, but it saves a lot of time and money. (The purist, however, may prefer to avoid walk cycles entirely.)

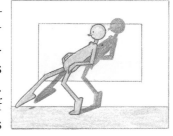

In a walk cycle, the two extreme positions are basically tracebacks of each other. There is, however, a slight difference: although they are in identical positions in relation to their screen location, in drawing 1 the right foot is trailing, and in drawing 9 it is forward.

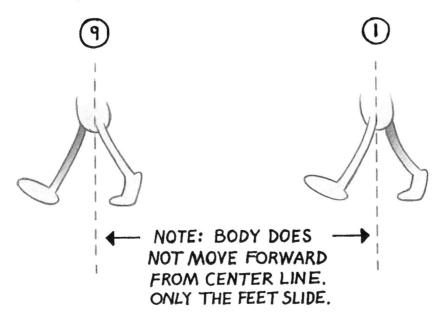

NOTE: BODY DOES NOT MOVE FORWARD FROM CENTER LINE. ONLY THE FEET SLIDE.

For the passing position, the body is merely raised vertically, while the foot is slid back along the ground to the midway position. The free leg is positioned as in a normal passing position. Remember that the body is merely moving vertically up and down (not forward), while the contact foot is slid back midway.

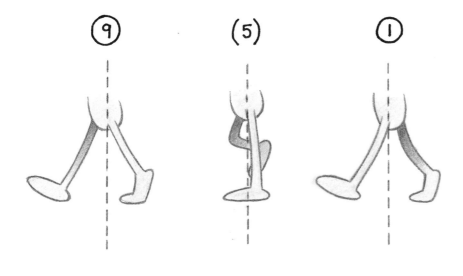

Now the inbetween positions are put in, based on the same principles. The body of drawing 3 is midway between 1 and (5), while the foot slides back to midway between the two. Remember, however, that the toe of the free leg is still in contact with the ground, so it, too, must slide back the same distance that the contact foot is moved.

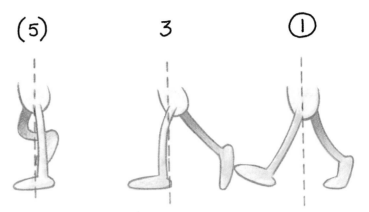

Similarly, drawing 7 is placed between (5) and 9. This time, however, the heel of the free leg must contact the ground ahead of the heel in extreme 9 (the same amount as the slide-back distance on the contact foot).

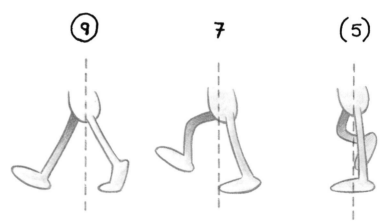

The cycle is completed by inbetweening 9 back to 1. All positions are identical to those of 3, (5), and 7, but this time the left foot is the free-leg foot.

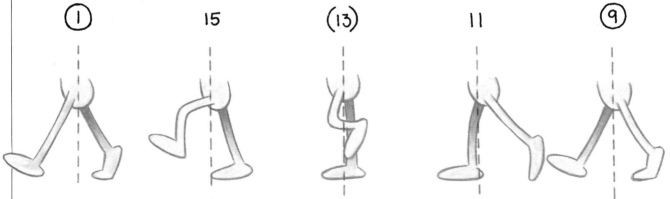

After the cycle is completed, it can be filmed (on twos) over and over again, with drawing 1 always following drawing 15 (1, 3, 5, 7, 9, 11, 13, 15, 1, 3, 5, 7, 9, 11, 13, 15, 1 . . .). You might want to try this on your own, using the walk cycle presented here.

Background Pans

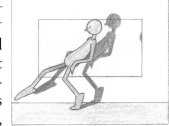

To complete the illusion of movement, the background has to be panned through the scene at identical distances to the slide distances of the contact foot, which should be equal in each drawing. The background pan, however, has to move in the reverse direction from that in which the character is walking. If, for instance, the character appears to walk from right to left, then the background must be panned from left to right.

Obviously, the background has to be specially lengthened to facilitate the panning. The number of frames in the scene and the distance moved in each frame will determine the exact length that it must be. If the pan is for 100 frames, for example, and each pan move is one-tenth of an inch, then the background must be long enough to pan 10 inches beyond its initial width.

When a pan is not correctly calculated, a kind of visual shudder—called strobing—appears on the screen. Strobing is likely to occur when a number of vertical lines appear on a background that is being panned from one side to another. Although everything else appears to move smoothly, the verticals seem to jump backward and forward—creating an irritating visual distraction for the audience. To avoid this, pans have to be shot on ones and should never move beyond a certain distance in each frame (usually about one-tenth of an inch is the maximum move per frame, although a fast zip pan can be much more). As a result, when a walk cycle is used with a background pan, the animation should be inbetweened on ones (the even numbers have to be added) so that it precisely matches the pan of the background.

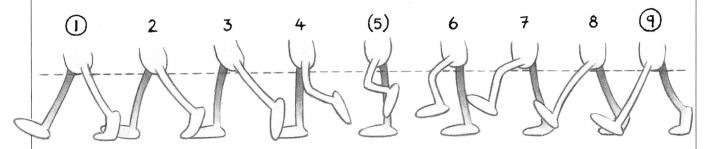

Remember: if the animation is shot on twos and the background is panned on ones, the animation will strobe and the foot will shudder in relation to the background contact point. If, on the other hand, the animation and the background are both shot on twos, the background will strobe. Hence, the need for inbetweens on ones for all walk cycles.

Frequently, a walk cycle has to be animated front on, rather than in profile. Sometimes it even has to be animated back on. With a front-on walk cycle, you use the same principles as with a profile walk, but you must think a little more when applying them. For a start, always keep the principles of perspective in mind when attempting a front-on walk cycle. If, for example, the character's step moves from 1 to 9, the keys appear as:

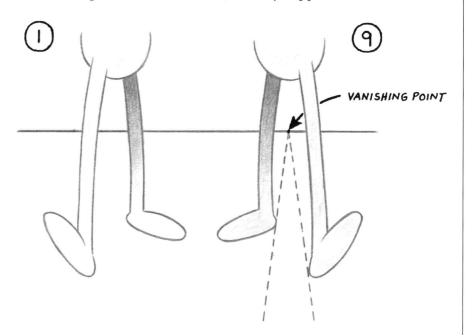

Notice how a point on the heel of each foot follows a line of perspective, which converges on the vanishing point on the horizon. If the walk is to be effective, any slip of the contact leg between the two key positions must follow this line of perspective. With this in mind, apply the same principles as you would for the profile walk to get the passing position:

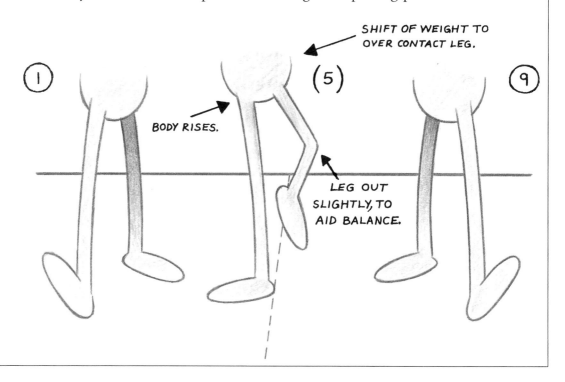

Then the inbetweens are added.

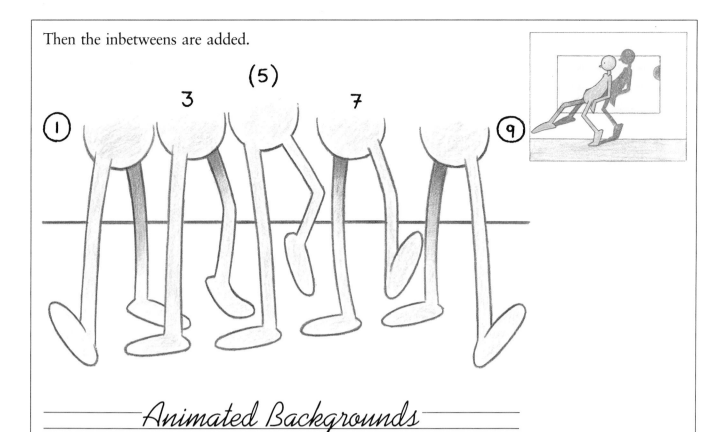

Animated Backgrounds

As you will remember, for a profile walk to be acceptable, the background has to pan at exactly the same speed as the slide of the contact foot; this is best achieved by putting both the pan and cycle on ones. The same principle applies to front-on walks, except that for these walks the background cannot be panned. Instead, the background must be animated, shrinking in perspective as it moves into the distance. This requires much more work, but if it's well done it is very effective.

The basic rule is the same—however far the contact foot slides on the cycle, the background objects must travel the same distance when they move in the background animation. If there is a stone on the ground next to the contact foot on the first key, it must remain on all the inbetween drawings, right through to the next key, and beyond.

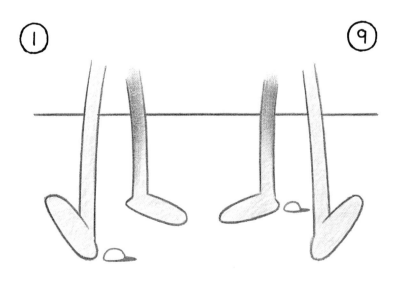

This rule applies to everything in the background, not just to objects that are close to the contact foot. Obviously, animating the entire background can be both time-consuming and expensive. It is advisable, if possible, to use a cycle of action that can be repeated ad infinitum. For example, a path with a line of telegraph poles along one side is a repeatable design to work with, as is a railroad track or a road with a broken line down the center. Bear in mind, however, that when you are inbetweening such an image in perspective, it is not sufficient to just draw a line exactly between two diminishing key positions—such as two telegraph poles.

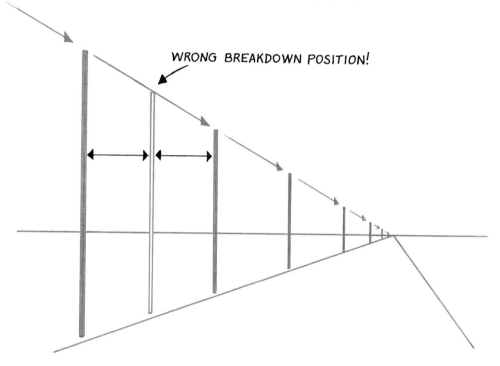

Instead, the inbetweens must reflect the fact that as the poles recede from the viewer, they appear closer together.

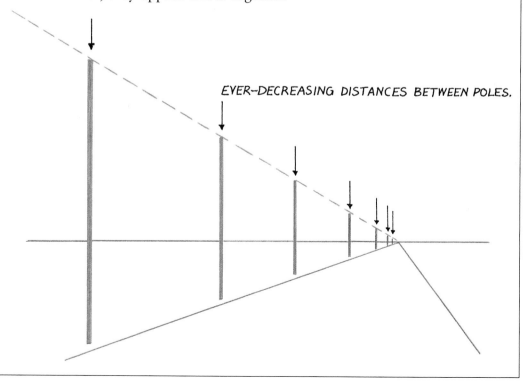

The inbetweens, therefore, must never be central, but should be somewhere nearer the second key position than the first. To position the inbetweens accurately, a simple technique has been devised. Lightly draw a diagonal between the top of the pole in key 1 and the bottom of the pole in key 9. Also draw a line from the top of the pole in key 9 to the bottom of the pole in key 1. Where these diagonal lines cross, draw a vertical line. The top of this vertical line is determined by the hypothetical line linking the tops of the poles in both keys, while its bottom falls on the line linking the bottoms of the poles in both keys. Now you have the position and height of the breakdown drawing. The inbetweens can be similarly placed.

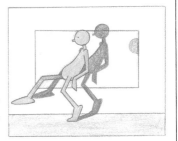

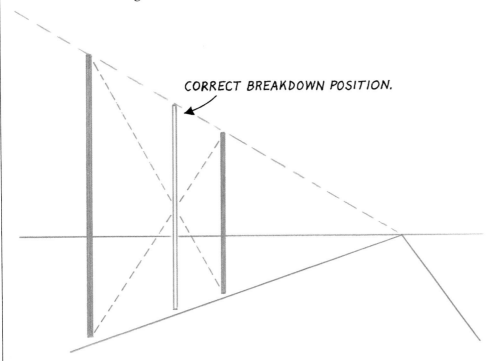

CORRECT BREAKDOWN POSITION.

Adding the Arms

Returning to the walk itself, you may wonder how to animate the rest of the body so that the whole figure is in movement. The most important thing to remember in all standard walks is that if the left leg is forward, the right arm is forward to counterbalance it (see drawing 1). Similarly, if the right leg is forward, the left arm is forward (see drawing 9). Following all the principles you used to inbetween the legs, you can now produce a passing position for the whole body. (First, slowly act it out yourself so you feel the action.) The passing position is roughly this:

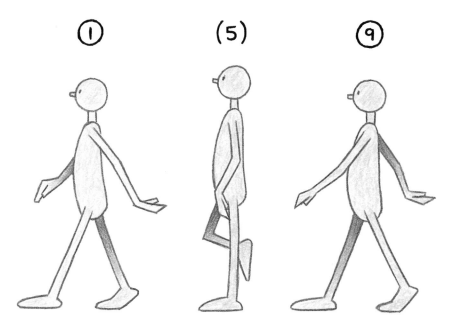

From the passing position, the inbetweens 3 and 7 can be produced, completing one step.

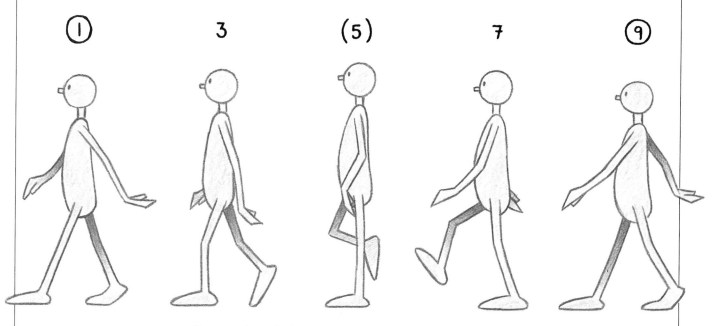

Repeat the whole procedure—using the opposite arm and leg positions—to obtain the other step.

Introducing Personality

Although you can now draw the basic standard walk, it is still rigid and mechanical, without personality. To make it more human, you must look more closely at the walk in action. Next time you are on a busy street, carefully observe people as they pass by. They all follow the basic pattern of movement that's been described, but notice how they differ in their execution of this standard movement. You may see a young girl taking short, sharp, perky strides, while an elderly, arthritic woman limps slowly, with her weight principally to one side. Or a young boy may swing his arms vigorously as he almost marches beside his mother, who is loaded with shopping bags and hardly moves her arms at all. Compare the clipped walk of a businessman with the uncoordinated meandering of a drunk. The more you look, the more you will realize that although everyone follows a basic pattern of movement, no two people have the same walk. Their size, weight, personality, speed, and psychological and physical well-being all contribute to making their walking movements unique.

Obviously, no animator—however experienced—can offer a formula that covers every conceivable style of walk. A few rudimentary guidelines, however, will give you clues about how to approach different walking movements. For example, instead of using the conventional passing position, many of the great animators of the past bent the knee of the free leg inward or outward.

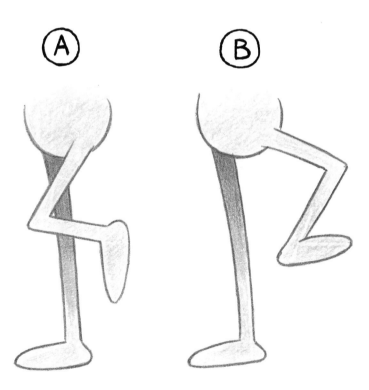

Experiment with this and then explore some variations. You might, for example, turn both knees inward on the keys and passing positions—1, (5), and 9—and outward on the inbetweens—3 and 7. This should give a shaky-legs look to the walk.

Or, instead of drawing the body up on the passing positions and down on the keys, break the rules and draw the body down on the passing position and up on the keys. The combinations are endless. But always remember that—whatever you do—the anatomy of the character cannot change. Legs do not shrink or stretch. If you want the body down, the legs must bend at the knee joints. If you want the body to rise above a straight-leg position, the character has to rise on tiptoe. All the options of squash and stretch (see pages 108–109) are open to you, as long as you respect the character's anatomy.

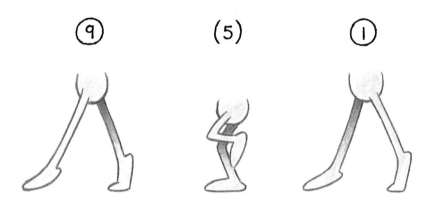

The Double-Bounce Walk

Can you recall Mickey Mouse's walk, and the way he seems to bounce up and down midstride? This is known as the double-bounce walk. Basically, it is simple to do, although the Disney animators elaborated on it for Mickey. Essentially, the double-bounce walk looks like this:

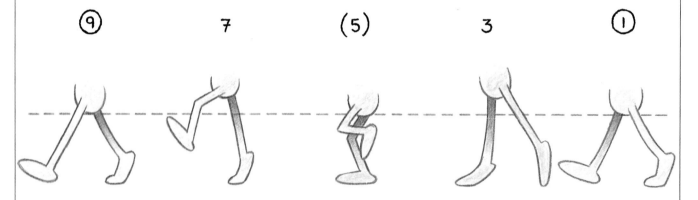

As you can see, the keys and the passing position are down, but the in-betweens are up. Note the bent knees on the down positions and the straight legs on tiptoe on the up positions. To compare effects, try putting the keys and passing position in the up position and the inbetweens in a down position.

In addition to varying body movements, you can add different head, leg, and arm positions. The variations can be stunning. And the more you try, the more you will learn.

Additional variations in the walking action may be created by altering the timing. Until now, a simple, even chart between the two keys has been used for the timing.

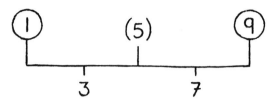

When this walk is filmed, it is extremely fast—and uninspiring. By just changing the charting and the number of inbetweens, you can profoundly affect the nature of a walk. If you want to keep the walk fast, you might try:

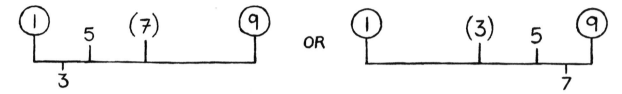

If you want a slower walk, you can add inbetweens and vary the charting accordingly.

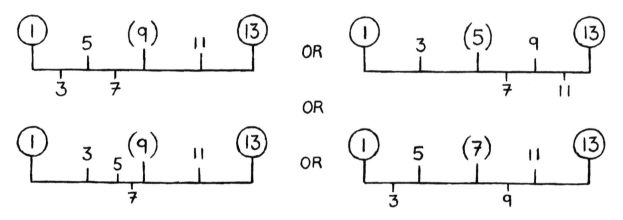

There is no limit to the variations you can make in the charting, the number of inbetweens, or the drawings themselves. It is entirely up to you, bearing in mind the demands of the scene, or the director.

At this point you may ask: How many frames should a walk take? There is no easy answer to this question. A chirpy, nervous character, for example, will walk much faster than a slow, ponderous character. Everything is relative. As a general rule of thumb, however, a stereotyped "basic" walk can usually be drawn over eight frames of film per step.

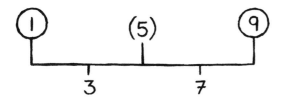

A more natural, yet fast, walk can be drawn over twelve frames. (Remember: the faster the walk you are attempting, the *fewer* drawings you need—and the slower the walk, the *more* drawings you need.)

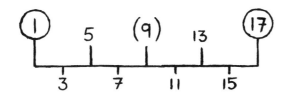

A natural, easy, man's walk can be drawn over sixteen frames.

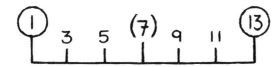

A natural, but fast, woman's walk could work effectively drawn over eight frames, although, again, the demands of the scene would dictate this.

To get more subtlety and fluidity into your walks, there are other points to consider. In all the illustrations so far, we have considered the body as more or less an oval with matchstick arms and legs stuck on. In reality, however, the human body is quite flexible, with rotating and bending joints. Consider the two key step positions, when seen in a more natural form.

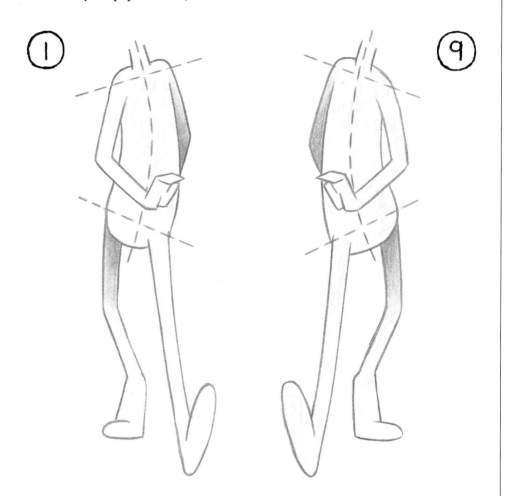

Notice (in key 1) that when the character's left leg is down and forward, the left hip is also down and forward, but the right hip is pulled up and back. The right arm, in compensation, drags the right shoulder down and forward, while the left is pulled up and back—resulting in a twist in the spine. In key 9, the reverse is true. Although this example is grossly exaggerated, in the course of one step a great deal of body movement goes on. As with all animation, you will learn only by feeling the movement in your own body, then re-creating it in drawn movement on your lightbox.

As you study body movement, don't forget the movement of the head. An enthusiastic character, for example, may sway the head from side to side while walking. Again, observe people on the street to fill your mental filing cabinet.

As you become more experienced with walks, take on the challenge of originality. Provided you get the basic principles of movement correct, there is no end to the sophistication and detail you can add to produce that little something special in the action.

Assignment

Copy and inbetween the key positions here on even inbetweens and shoot on twos for six feet. Then, using the same two key positions (and with as many inbetweens as you choose), create your own walk cycle encompassing as many of the guidelines from this chapter as you can. Shoot for a minimum of four seconds (or longer, if your cycle is a long, slow one).

Study every aspect of your walk cycle and see where improvements could be made. If you feel confident enough, make the necessary changes and reshoot. Then compare the difference between your first tests and your second. Repeat this process, if necessary.

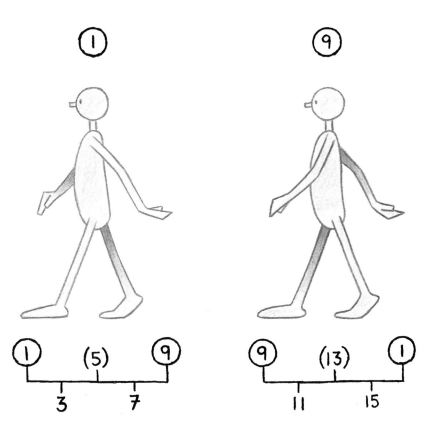

RUNS

COMPARING RUNS AND WALKS
ANTICIPATION

A

run is—in essence—a faster, more dynamic version of a walk.

Comparing Runs and Walks

Everything that applies to a walk, applies to a run—only more so. The up-and-down movement of the walk is exaggerated in the run to give it more snap. This is because in a run the body is not so much lifted by the straight leg of the passing position (as it is in a walk), but is more driven upward by the push-off of the key contact foot.

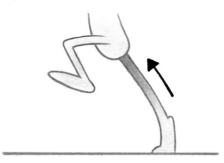

In a run the arms move more vigorously than in a walk, because they are responsible for driving the legs into action. Olympic sprinters, for example, are not so much trained to move their legs faster as to punch their arms faster—which, in turn, prompt the legs to move quickly. Also, in a sprint, the arms punch hard in a bent position, for added speed. This is because a bent arm is a shorter lever to move, and—as scientists and engineers know—the shorter the lever, the faster it can be moved.

Also, because you are trying to obtain more forward momentum in a run than a walk, the body lean is much more pronounced.

One final pointer for a run is that, in contrast to a walk, the stride covers a lot of ground—more than the legs can reach in a natural stride position with both feet on the ground.

Obviously, drawing a run demands more thought than drawing a walk, but fewer drawings! The track-and-field definition of a walk is that one foot must be in contact with the ground at any one moment. In a run, however, both feet lose contact with the ground for most of the stride.

A run can be drawn in as few as three drawings. This is crude, however, and too fast—and it is rarely convincing unless the scene requires a kind of furious, scrabbling run.

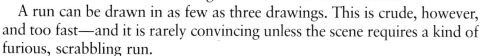

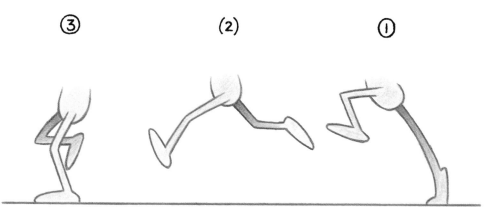

Like walks, runs have their own personalities, depending on the requirements of the scene, the psychological state of the character, and even on the texture of the surface on which the character is running. Consider, for instance, the difference in running styles for a sprint and a marathon. The sprinter uses short, sharp, explosive movements—caring little for preserving stamina. The marathon runner, however, sacrifices speed for economy and runs in a far more relaxed, economic, upright style.

Where the figure is running is another consideration. If the figure is running downhill, he will lean back slightly and open his arms more, to help brake his speed. If he is running uphill, however, he will lean forward and drive his arms harder, to give him the added impetus to get up the hill.

It all depends on what the running figure has to contend with. With any run, however, the contact foot drives the character up and forward far more than is necessary on any walk. Therefore, the key position has to be dynamic. In other words, the driving-off position must have thrust and direction. Consider these two drawings as an example of a sprinter's action.

Obviously drawing B is more *dynamic*. It is stronger, has direction, and shows that the character really knows where he is going. The first is weak and uncoordinated; it looks more like a stumbling, exhausted marathon runner at the end of a race than a purposeful, explosive sprinter. The way the key positions in a run are drawn says everything about the type of run.

Look at drawing B again. It's worth noting that in a run—unlike a walk—the body weight is way ahead, out of balance with the contact foot. This communicates that the character either has to get the other foot beneath him fast or he will fall flat on his face. Here, then, is another secret of a good run—constantly avoiding a fall by rushing the feet through beneath the body weight. Generally, the faster the run, the greater the lean.

The next key position in the run is the equivalent of the stride position in the walk. In a run, however, this is the point where there is no contact with the ground. The drive from the contact foot causes the body to rise, while the free leg is moving through quickly to contact the ground. The stride position in a run may therefore appear like this:

The third key position is the contact position. The contact leg is now bent to cushion the weight of the body coming down again, and therefore there is a slight sinking of the whole body. The far arm is already driving through, anticipating the left leg swinging through for the next step.

If these key positions for a fast run are put into a run cycle, they look like this:

Since a run is fast, it will always look best inbetweened on ones—particularly if it is a run cycle matched to a panning background. Indeed, it is almost a rule that all runs should be shot on ones.

Newton's third law of motion states that "for every action there is an equal and opposite reaction." Anticipation, for the animator, represents this law in operation. When animating any major action in a scene, it is always necessary to anticipate the action before initiating it. If a character is going to run off-screen-left from a standing start, it is first necessary to give him a short movement to screen-right to anticipate it.

This is often seen in Disney or Warner Brothers cartoons, where the main character sees another character and speeds off after him. You always see a static pose (1), followed by a wind-up anticipation (2), and then a fast scurry, or run (3), out of shot. Actually, if the anticipation is convincing enough, you can dispense with the run stage altogether and just pop the character off the picture. This effect can be further enhanced if objects in the background are sucked out of shot in the wake of the off-screen character. But remember that the anticipation must be convincing to the audience. For the anticipation to be effective in this case, the character must keep his eyes set in exactly the direction in which he intends to run. If he does not do this, the audience will not know what he has in mind before he disappears.

A perfect example of anticipation in action is a sprinter at the starting blocks. Note that as he is in the set position, and the gun goes off, he moves back slightly before moving forward on "go."

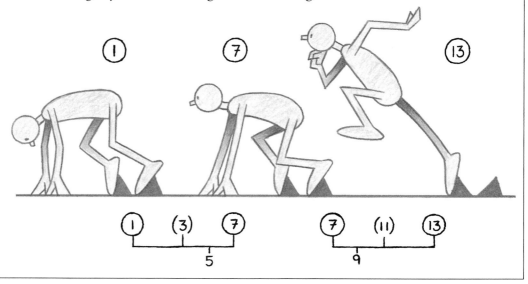

Anticipation will work for any action, not just a run. If a character looks up, he should momentarily look down first. If he jumps, there should be a little squash before he takes off. If he talks, there should be a little anticipation in the face or head before he begins.

Assignment

Copy the standing-figure key provided and animate him into a run off to screen-left (his right)—remembering all the principles of anticipation. Then, walk the character in from screen-right (his left) and have him stop (using the key position provided), look around, pause, and then run off again.

REALISTIC TOUCHES

WEIGHT IN MOVEMENT
CARRYING A WEIGHT
ANTICIPATION AND WEIGHT
FLEXIBILITY
OVERLAPPING ACTION

W eight, flexibility, and overlapping action are critical in making animation convincing.

If a run is to be convincing, the effect of weight must be considered. Basically, you must always remember that the larger the character, the more weight he has to carry. And the more weight that must be carried, the slower the character must move, and the harder it is for the character to control that weight. The animator, therefore, has far more to consider when drawing a fat man running than a thin man. It is perfectly acceptable for a thin, light character to almost skim across the ground. When it comes to the fat man, it's a different story.

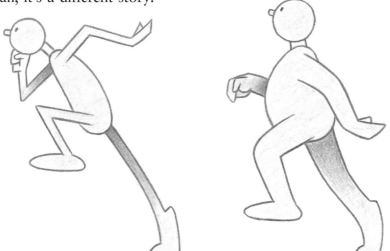

The simplest way to describe weight is with a bouncing rubber ball. Traditionally, a bouncing ball appears something like this:

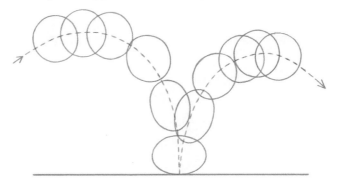

Note how the ball tends to squash when it hits the ground—losing its round shape—then elongates as it springs up and forward. These movements are quite fast (because of the speed and momentum of the descending

ball), but the movement tends to slow considerably as the ball reaches the highest position. At this high point, the ball reestablishes its normal shape—perfectly round—before descending again, and distorting slightly once more, due to the drag caused by its acceleration.

With a much lighter ball—perhaps a ping-pong ball—the action differs.

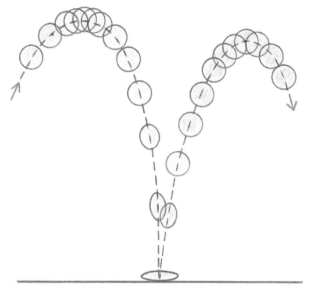

Notice that the ball moves very fast on the bounce, yet hovers at the top of the bounce. This is because the air tends to hold the light ball up longer, and when it hits, it is easily catapulted upward again, the force of gravity hardly affecting it.

On the other hand, if a heavy ball, such as a cannonball, were to bounce, there would be a very different effect.

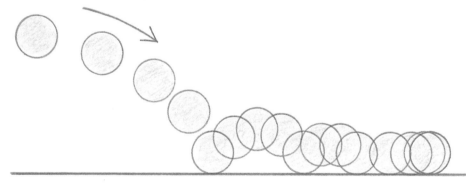

Here the force of gravity pulls heavily on the cannonball and little bounce occurs. Instead, the ball quickly comes to rest. And, because the ball is heavy and solid, it does not lose its shape when bouncing. Indeed, it is more likely that the ground will bend before the ball.

All the principles shown for the bouncing ball apply to everything that moves, and they are particularly useful for animating walks and runs.

When a character is carrying a heavy weight, his whole posture and way of moving change. A man carrying a sack of potatoes, for instance, will stand differently from a man who is empty-handed.

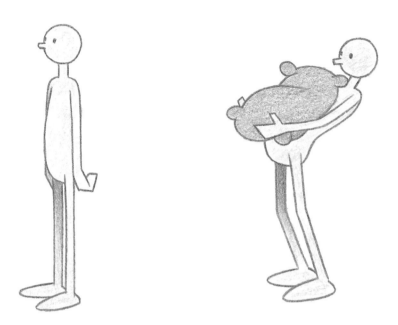

Notice the tremendous lean backward, which is necessary to compensate for the added weight so that the character appears balanced. If the man did not lean back, he would be pulled forward and would fall flat on his face. The general rule is that the more weight there is, the more the body position has to change to compensate for it. If the weight is tremendously heavy, then a bend in the legs may also be necessary to accentuate the illusion of great weight.

Now when the character begins to move, his speed and action are affected. The heavier the weight, the slower the movement will tend to be. In this case, the man will have to walk quite slowly because he has a great deal of extra weight to move and his muscles are not accustomed to the added load. The muscles must work much harder, against added resistance, and as a result will appear more labored in their movement.

When moving weight, it is essential to remember that the greater the weight, the greater the resistance that gravity will apply to that weight. If the man is trying to move the weight, plus his body, up and forward—as at the beginning of a step—then the initial movement will be extremely difficult and slow. When, however, he has the momentum going to move the weight, it will be easier for him to maintain, or increase, the speed. And if he is moving the weight downward, gravity will actually help him and the action will accelerate.

When walking, therefore, the man carrying the sack will start extremely slowly, and only really be able to speed up when he gains momentum. An approximate breakdown of his first step might be as follows (although this will vary, depending on the demands of the action you are attempting):

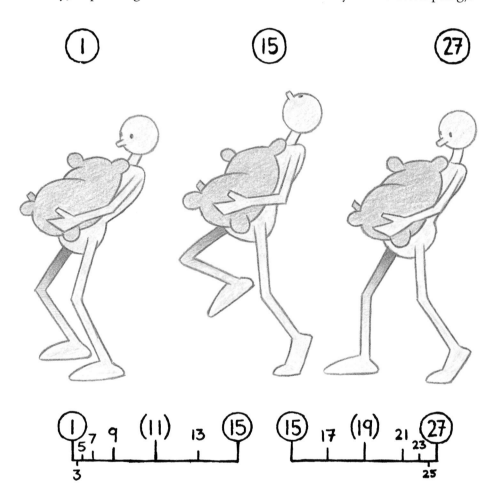

Note, first, that this walk is extremely slow because a great weight is involved. Second, there tends to be a tremendous slow-out from key number 1, as the man struggles to get the weight moving. There is also a slight slow-in to key number 27 as the man, having gotten the momentum going, must attempt to slow it down to some degree as he prepares to push off on the next step. This is another feature of weight—if the character did not attempt to slow down in this way, the weight would come crashing to the ground under the force of momentum and gravity.

Obviously, many other factors influence the action. For example, is the man big in proportion to the weight, or is he small? Or, whatever his size, is he strong or weak in his ability to handle the weight? Indeed, so many factors occur when dealing with weight in action that it is impossible to offer concrete formulas to cover every eventuality. If, however, the basic principles of weight are understood, they can be applied to a variety of situations.

What will happen to the walk if, for example, the man is carrying the sack under one arm? First, his posture will change considerably. Instead of a backward lean, he will need much more of a sideways lean to compensate for the heavy weight. His free arm is held out, to give added compensation to the extra weight, and his legs have a less symmetrical stance.

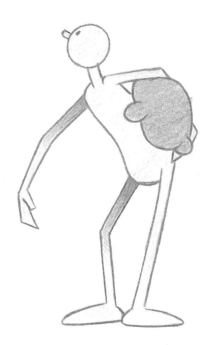

The walk, then, will be extremely exaggerated, with a kind of dragging, limping movement—in order for the added side weight to be brought around and forward on every step that the weighted leg takes. Act it out yourself, and you will begin to get the feel of what is needed. If you can feel it, you have a far greater chance of producing it on the screen.

Anticipation and Weight

When moving great weight, remember to use anticipation. If your character is attempting to throw the sack into the back of a truck, then it will be far more convincing if he puts one, or two, little back swings in before he throws the sack forward.

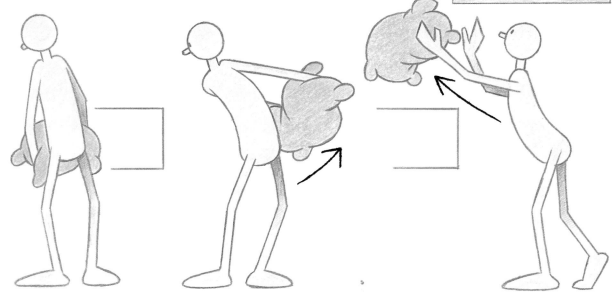

Similarly, if a character is sitting down and has to get up and move forward, a little backward lean of the body will make it more convincing.

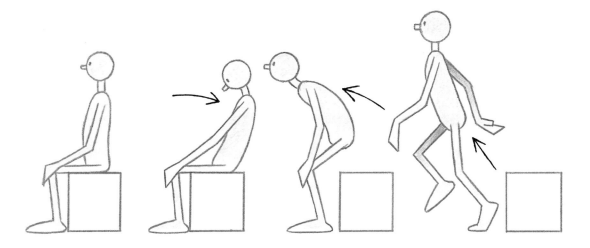

Obviously, if the character is fat, old, or weak, this type of anticipation will be pronounced. On the other hand, if the character is quick and nimble, the anticipation does not have to be so strong. Act the movement out before you try to animate it. Or get someone else to act it out and watch him or her a few times before you begin to draw.

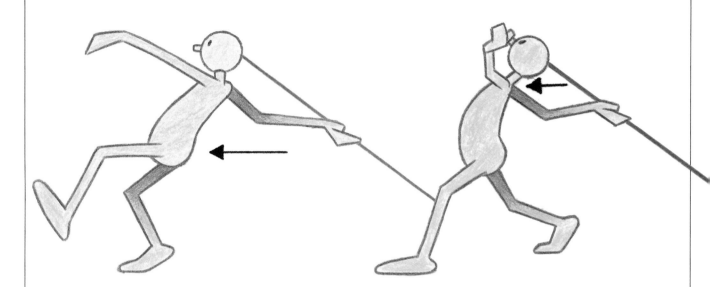

Flexibility of the joints is essential to good animation. Stiffness is the hallmark of poor animation technique. The more flexibility that can be put into an animated movement (without the character actually looking like rubber), the more convincing it will be. A favorite phrase of older animators is "successive breaking of joints." Quite simply, this means that, as in overlapping action, not all parts of the action move at the same time; instead, a succession of movements takes place in any action. This is particularly true of the human body.

When contemplating an action, the animator must first ascertain which body part is leading the action and which part is following through. A classic example of this can be seen in the javelin thrower. Experienced

javelin coaches always emphasize that there is more to javelin throwing than just running and throwing. Apart from the fast run up, they emphasize that at the end of the run the feet should be planted in a solid, steady position with the hips driven forward and the javelin arm held well back. From this powerful hip position, the throw unwinds from a series of movements, which bear a strong resemblance to the whip action from the center to the upper tip of an archery bow.

The body arches from the hip and the shoulder moves forward, ahead of the body. Then the elbow moves forward, to be followed by the wrist. Finally, the javelin is released, with the fingertips following through at the last moment. This is a perfect example of a successive breaking of joints.

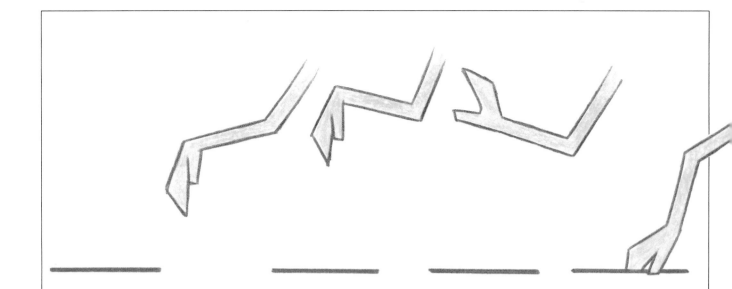

Every action has some breaking of joints, regardless of how dynamic it is. In animation, the simple act of picking up a pencil appears far more flexible, or fluid, just by successively breaking the joints.

Although the action is exaggerated in the example, observe how it goes through a series of changes of direction in the joints of the arm and hand, and the way it starts at the elbow and seems to ripple along to the hand, rather like a whip cracking. Note, too, that after a joint has led by breaking in one direction, it immediately breaks back to allow the next joint to lead

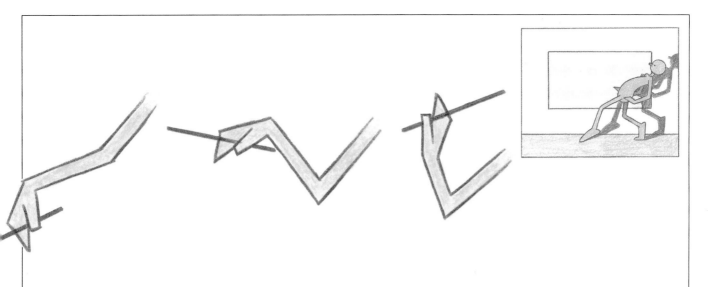

the next part of the sequence. That joint, in turn, breaks back, making way for the next one.

When breaking joints, however, you must always remember the limitations of human anatomy. Never overextend the bend of the joints into impossible positions. Effective animation uses successive breaking of joints to add flexibility. A less-than-subtle use of this technique, however, may render the action unbelievable. Beware of excess, unless the scene specifically demands it.

Overlapping Action

In addition to weight, you must consider overlapping action, which is the effect of a main movement on parts that are secondary to the main movement. If, for example, a hand is waving a flag, the moving hand is the main action, but the flag follows on, secondary to it. If the hand changes direction, the flag continues along its path of movement until it reaches its full length, then it again follows the hand, until the movement changes.

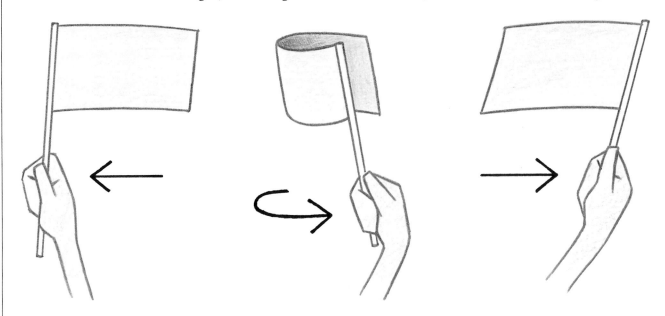

Overlapping applies to almost everything and can be used to great effect in all animation scenes. Clothing, for instance, provides an excellent example of overlapping action. If a character wearing a coat is walking along, the coat will seem to drag against the direction in which the character is walking. If the character suddenly stops, the coat will tend to continue, then slowly fall back into a static position. Hair, scarves, floppy sweaters—anything that is free-moving yet attached to the main body of movement—may move as a result of overlapping action.

Assignment

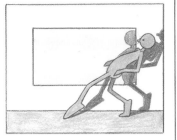

Copying the key drawing below, animate the character up from his seated position. Make him bend over and pick up the ball, then throw the ball out of the screen. Finally, exit the character from the scene in any way that occurs to you.

Technical Information

earning the technical aspects
of animation is extremely
important if the action is to
be viewed to maximum effect.

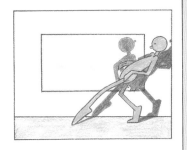

The dope sheet, or camera instruction sheet, makes it possible for you to organize your thinking in relation to your proposed animation and for the cameraman to accurately chart your wishes. At first glance the dope sheet appears to be a formidable adversary, with a mass of intersecting lines indicating apparent confusion. The dope sheet can, however, be broken down into quite simple section headings. Every horizontal line, for example, represents one frame of film. There are 16 frames of action for every foot of 35mm film; therefore, every sixteenth horizontal line is printed thicker to indicate each foot of film. And, when you know that (with the exception of some TV systems) there are 24 frames of action projected every second, you can visualize each foot and a half of lines as one second of screen time.

☐ The vertical divisions are a little more complicated, but are easy to understand when taken in simple order. Refer to the illustration on page 89. The column on the far left is used by the animator to scribble down any thoughts about the action visualized for the scene. These notes are solely for the animator's benefit—reminders of what he or she wants the action to do at a particular frame of film.

▨ The next column, to the right, is the dialogue column. Here all the dialogue is marked (phonetically) in relation to the frame of action with which it coincides in the film. Alternatively, if music synchronization is necessary for the action, the music beat and principal sounds are indicated in this column.

▨ The next six columns are concerned with the various cel levels of animation—or levels of acetate—to be shot. Often an animation scene is built up of several levels, so this is where the animator indicates the precise order in which they are to be shot—the lowest level in the right-hand column, the highest to the left. As you can see, there are five levels to play with, plus a background artwork level. It is preferable for the animation to take place on only one or two levels, because the more levels of acetate used, the greater the loss of light and color intensity. Five tends to be the maximum number of workable levels.

▨ In the column on the far right labeled "Camera Instructions," the animator writes any specific instructions (such as field size and truck and panning movements) for the cameraman. This information must be clearly and precisely written; any inaccuracy will result in misunderstanding by the cameraman and potential mistakes in filming.

▨ Finally, at the top of the dope sheet, the animator writes in the sequence and scene number on the left and the sheet number on the right. (Almost invariably the animator is working on a scene that lasts for more than one page in length, so each additional page has to be numbered in successive order.) The space in the middle—between the scene box and the sheet box—is usually used to write in the title of the scene concerned.

The example shows the dope sheet for a simple scene—entitled "A New Day"—of one level of animation (plus a background) to be filmed on twos (one drawing for every two frames).

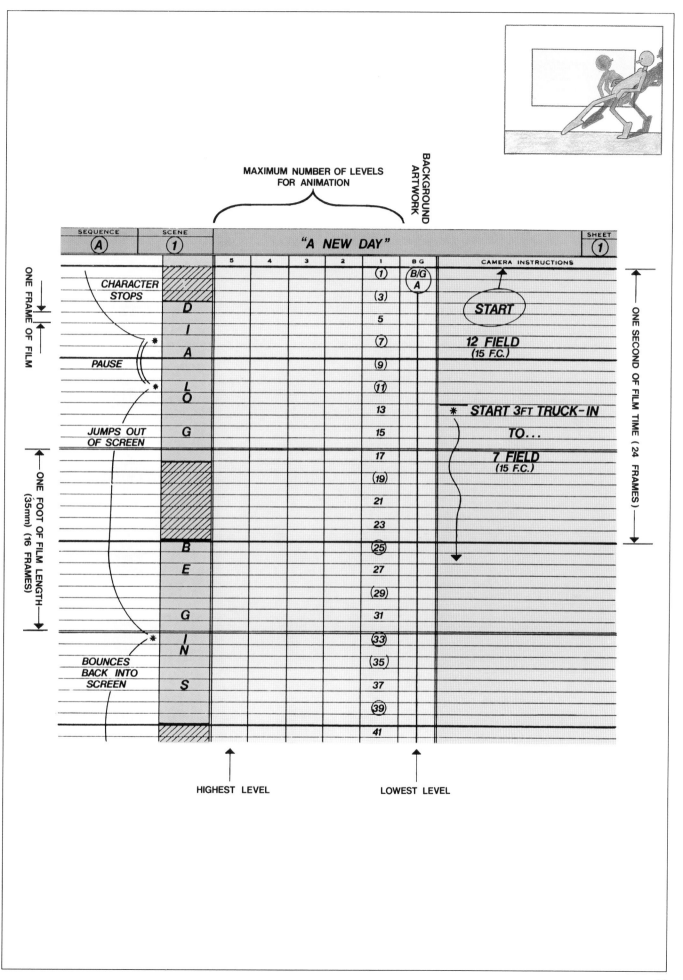

Field Size

The area of the picture that is framed by the camera when a scene is being shot is known as the field size. The field size can be anything the animator chooses, but the standard sizes are 12 and 15 fields. A 12-field measures 12 inches from the extreme left side to the extreme right side of the artwork, with a height of approximately 8.75 inches from top to bottom. This ratio—called the standard Academy field ratio—is the one used in most films. Television also uses the Academy ratio for its screen dimensions. A 15-field measures 15 inches horizontally and is approximately 10.9 inches from top to bottom.

Field sizes can, however, be as variable as the technical versatility of camera used for shooting the artwork. Usually a rostrum camera can focus in as close as 2 inches wide, or can pull back to a 40-inch span, or more in

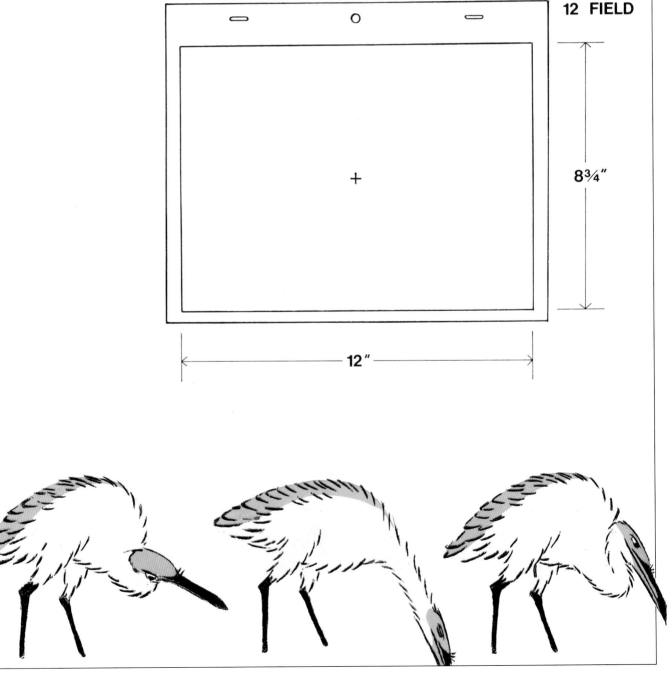

12 FIELD

8¾″

12″

some cases. When you are using a field larger than a standard 15, however, everything moving in the shot has to be animated on cels that are larger than the largest standard-size cels available from most animation supply stores. These large-size cels thus have to be specially cut and punched, a process that is not only costly, but can prove technically troublesome as well. For example, when large cel areas are repeatedly placed on the relatively small registration peg holes, there can be so much cel wobble or slippage that the animation, when filmed, may appear to be jiggling around against the fixed background. To avoid this, it is necessary to strengthen the peg holes with specially designed peg reinforcements, or to punch a series of extended holes along the entire edge of the animation cel.

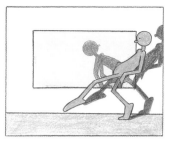

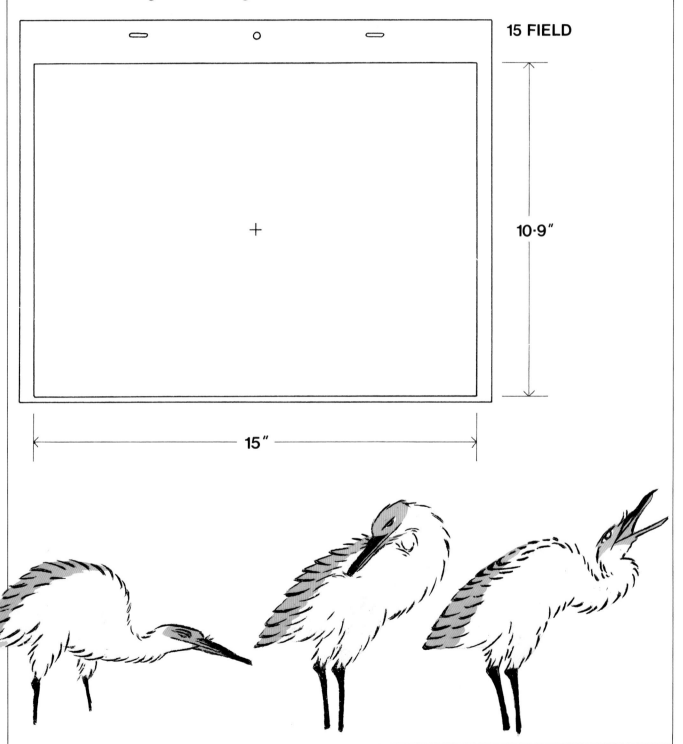

15 FIELD

10·9″

15″

Wide-Screen and Cinemascope

In addition to the standard Academy field ratio, there are two principal ratio systems used for cinematic projection—wide-screen and cinemascope, or scope, for short. Wide-screen uses the Academy format for its horizontal dimension, but crops the vertical top-to-bottom measurement, producing a slightly squatter format. A 15-inch field size, which is the preferable size to use in large-screen cinema projection, would thus be 15 inches wide but approximately 8.1 inches from top to bottom.

15 FIELD WIDE-SCREEN

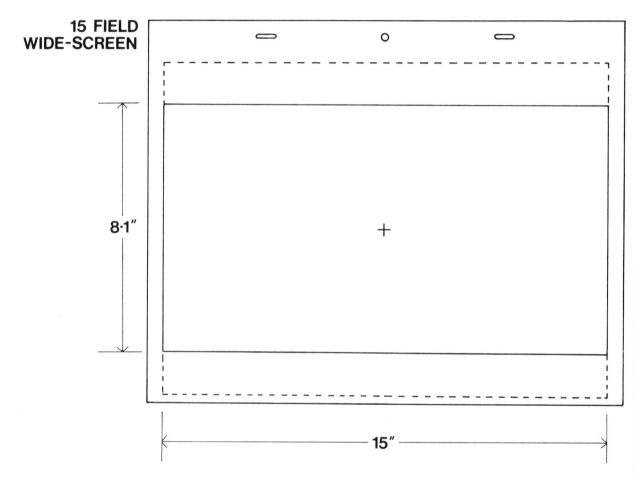

8·1"

15"

Cinemascope uses an entirely different system from the standard Academy, in that artwork is shot and projected through a special lens, known as an anomorphic lens. This lens squeezes the image inward from side to side, resulting in a squeezed image on the film frame; then stretches it out again when projected onto a screen. The screen ratio for scope animation is even squatter than wide-screen. The dimensions are 15 inches horizontally and, approximately, 6 to 7 inches vertically. Projected, the scope system produces the most impressive and spectacular effects in filmmaking, but it is extremely difficult, or unsatisfactory, to show on a standard Academy TV screen—a very important economic consideration these days, especially with the new, lucrative video markets.

Wide-screen has a definite advantage, in that it can be satisfactorily viewed in both systems if, when designing and animating the film, the full Academy field is drawn and shot—with the projector gate cropping the top and bottom of the shot when the film is projected in a movie theater.

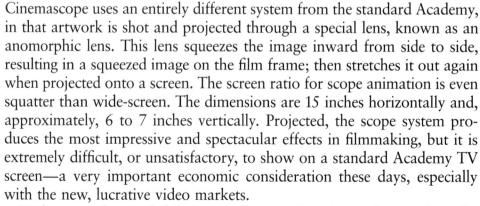

TV Cut-off and Safe-Titling

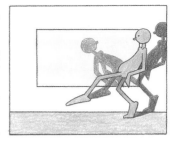

Today, most animation is produced for television, so strict attention must be paid to TV cut-off and TV safe-titling areas when planning a scene. TV cut-off is the area within the field size where the viewer's TV screen crops in from the edge of the shot, thereby concealing a certain amount of the scene. The cut-off varies from TV set to TV set, and from region to region, and therefore can never be predicted accurately. Nevertheless, an approximate maximum can be used as the norm for all layout purposes. In a 12-inch field, the amount cropped horizontally is approximately 3 inches (three fields)—1.5 inches from the left and 1.5 inches from the right of the screen. The vertical cut-off will be in accord with the standard Academy ratio's dimensions. The same applies to a 15-inch field, where the horizontal cut-off is approximately 4 inches (four fields)—2 inches from the left and 2 inches from the right side of the screen.

TV safe-titling is an even more extreme cut-off area. It indicates where important titling can be safely positioned without a fall-off or distortion effect from the curved TV screen edges. The TV safe-titling area falls approximately 1/2 inch from the left and the right sides of the TV cut-off area for both a 12-inch and 15-inch field size.

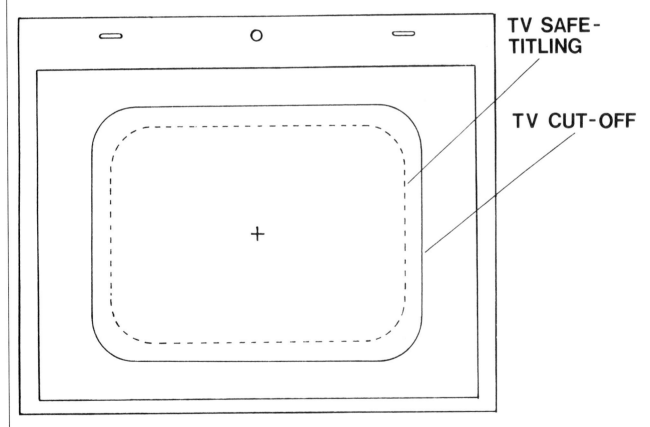

TV SAFE-TITLING

TV CUT-OFF

For television, all titles and supers (any lettering, logos, or graphics displayed over a frame of film) must fall within the TV safe-titling area. If however, the film is to be viewed only on a cinema screen, the titling may be positioned almost to the extreme edge of the relevant field size.

The Graticule

To make life simpler, the animator may buy a graticule, which makes it possible to work out field-size measurements far more efficiently. Basically, the graticule is a transparent grid with an outer dimension relating to the standard Academy screen ratio and a series of horizontal and vertical measurements moving toward a central point.

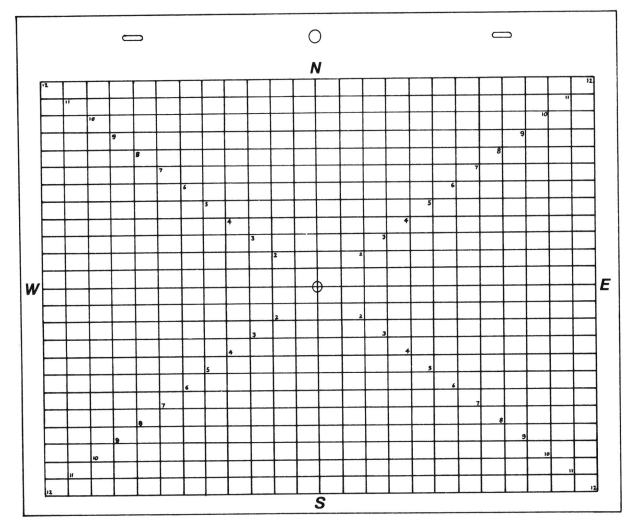

On most graticules, all the field sizes from 1 to 12 inches are clearly marked (1 to 15 on a 15-inch graticule), as well as the TV cut-offs for most field sizes. This makes it far easier to judge the field size of any animation. Also indicated on the graticule are four directional reference points—north, south, east, and west. These offer direction, if the chosen field size does not have the same center as the largest field on the graticule (12 or 15).

If, for example, you want to use an 8-field with the same center as the 12-field graticule, place a piece of clean paper on the registration pegs and over the graticule. Then, on a lightbox, simply trace the layout field size from the 8-inch corners on the graticule. If, however, your action is offset to the right of the central position and you want to place your 8-field two fields to the right of the center to feature it, mark the center point of the 8-field (two grids to the right of the 12-field graticule center) on your paper, then slide the paper across to the left so that the marked center lies directly on top of

the graticule center. Making sure that the paper is lined up perfectly square with the graticule edges, trace the 8-field. Then when you place the paper back on the pegs, you will see it indicates the 8-field two fields to the right of the 12-field center.

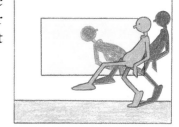

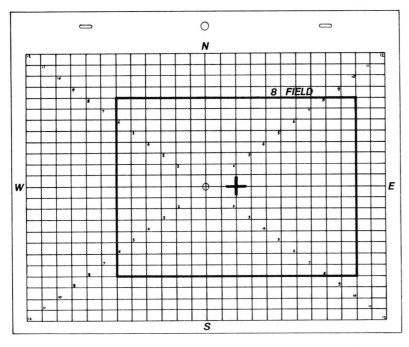

To indicate to the cameraman your exact position for the fielding, you write the following instructions in the far-right column of your dope sheet.

8 FIELD
$$\left(\begin{array}{c} \textbf{2 F EAST} \\ \textbf{12 F.C.} \end{array} \right)$$

This means that the camera is filming an 8-field which is two fields to the right (east) of the center of the 12-field graticule. If you wanted your 8-field two fields to the left of the same center, it would appear like this:

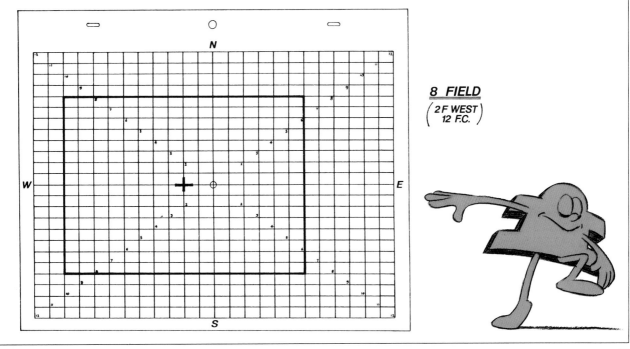

8 FIELD
$$\left(\begin{array}{c} \textbf{2 F WEST} \\ \textbf{12 F.C.} \end{array} \right)$$

Similarly, if you wanted a 4-field to be shot four fields above the center of a 15-field graticule, it would appear:

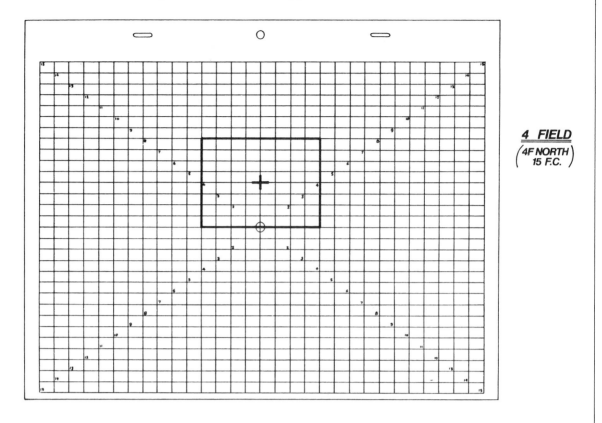

4 FIELD

$\left(\begin{array}{c} \text{4F NORTH} \\ \text{15 F.C.} \end{array}\right)$

If, however, you want your 4-field to be four fields above and four fields to the right of the center of the 15-field graticule, it would be written:

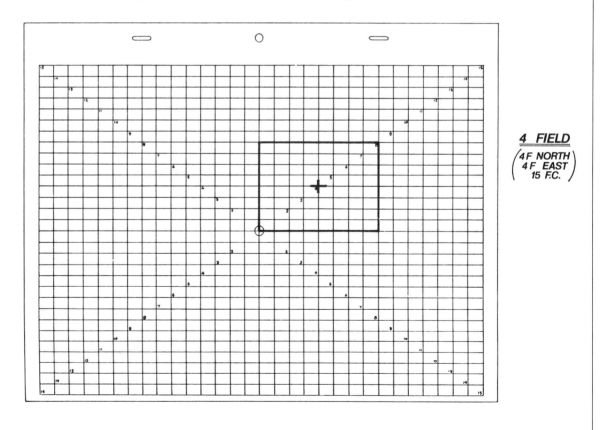

4 FIELD

$\left(\begin{array}{c} \text{4F NORTH} \\ \text{4F EAST} \\ \text{15 F.C.} \end{array}\right)$

All the graticule references are measured from the center position of what-ever graticule you are using (12 or 15). But remember that if your chosen field size overlaps the maximum size of the graticule field, then the paper and cel used for the animation have to be extra-large to avoid a cel edge appearing in the scene. You may, for example, want an 8-field to be six fields beneath a 12-field center.

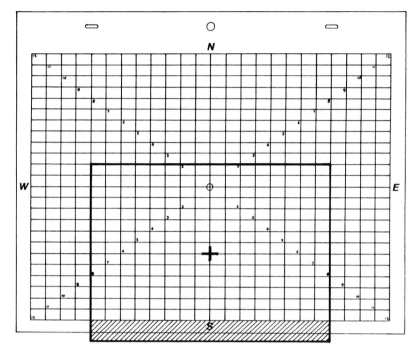

8 FIELD
$\left(\dfrac{6\,F\;SOUTH}{12\;F.C.}\right)$

The shaded area shows where extra paper or cel is needed to cover the field to avoid the edges showing on the screen. It is always advisable to draw a field guide on a piece of paper beforehand so that you know exactly where the camera will be, and where the animation should be drawn.

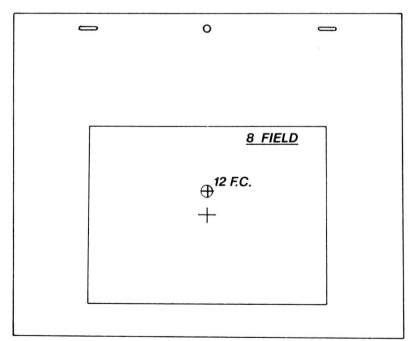

**ANIMATION
FIELD GUIDE**

8 FIELD
$\left(\dfrac{2\,F\;SOUTH}{12\;F.C.}\right)$

It is also advisable to include your field guide with the scene when sending it to the cameraman to avoid any confusion when the scene is shot.

Panning Guides

Whenever the camera will pan right or left (east or west) or up or down (north or south) during the animated action, the graticule is essential for working out the move for the cameraman. If, for instance, you start a scene on an 8-field eight fields west of a 12-field center, and want the camera to pan across—in three feet of film—to an 8-field eight fields east of the same center, you can draw the field guide to clarify the action area:

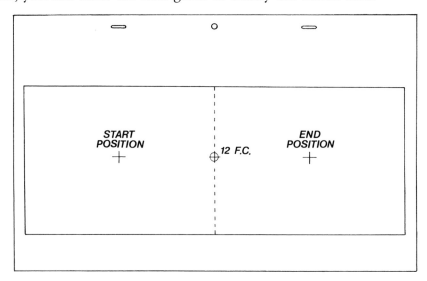

And dope the camera instructions as:

8 FIELD

$\left(\begin{array}{c}\underline{8\,F\ WEST}\\ 12\ F.C.\end{array}\right)$

START 3FT.
PAN EAST
TO...

8 FIELD

$\left(\begin{array}{c}\underline{8\,F\ EAST}\\ 12\ F.C.\end{array}\right)$

Or you may want the camera to move from a 4-field, eight fields south of a 12-field center, up to a 4-field, eight fields north of a 12-field center:

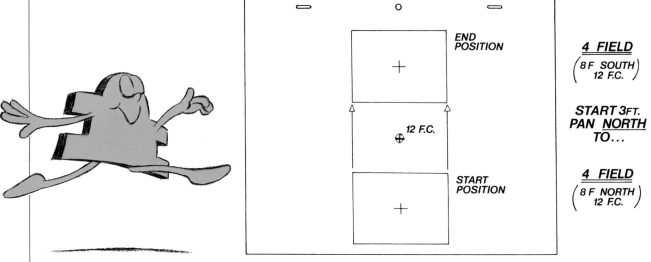

4 FIELD

$\left(\begin{array}{c}\underline{8\,F\ SOUTH}\\ 12\ F.C.\end{array}\right)$

START 3FT.
PAN NORTH
TO...

4 FIELD

$\left(\begin{array}{c}\underline{8\,F\ NORTH}\\ 12\ F.C.\end{array}\right)$

Sometimes, however, you may want to pan further east or west than is indicated on the graticule. In such situations, it is necessary to measure extra field positions and draw them on an extended paper field guide. If, for example, the scene starts on a 6-field, four fields west of a 12-field center, and pans east to a 6-field, twenty fields east of a 12-field center, then the field guide and doping would appear as:

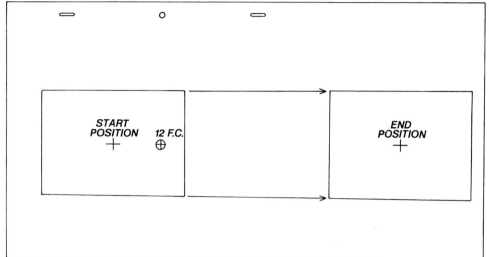

6 FIELD
$\left(\begin{array}{c}\text{4 F WEST}\\\text{12 F.C.}\end{array}\right)$

PAN EAST
IN 3 FT.
TO...

6 FIELD
$\left(\begin{array}{c}\text{20 F EAST}\\\text{12 F.C.}\end{array}\right)$

Instead of just panning from a field size in one position to the same field size in another position, you can pan from the first field size to a smaller—or larger—field size in another position. This is called a truck pan. If, for instance, you start on an 8-field, six fields east of a 15-field center, and want to move, in five feet of film, to a 4-field, nine fields west of a 15-field center, the truck pan field guide and doping will look like this:

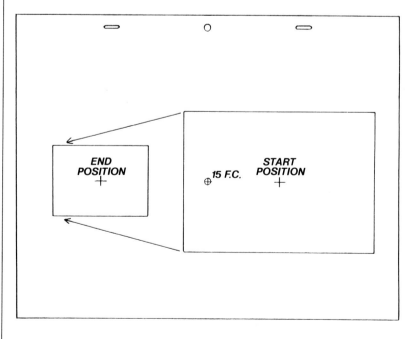

8 FIELD
$\left(\begin{array}{c}\text{6 F EAST}\\\text{15 F.C.}\end{array}\right)$

START 5 FT.
TRUCK/PAN
TO...

4 FIELD
$\left(\begin{array}{c}\text{9 F WEST}\\\text{15 F.C.}\end{array}\right)$

Alternatively, if you start on the 4-field and end up on the 8-field, the field guide and doping would appear as:

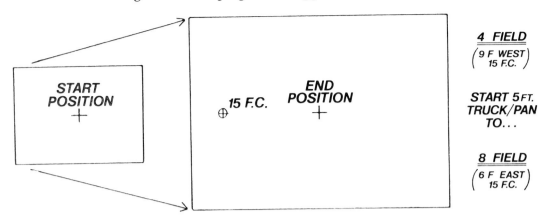

Remember that the field guide indicates where the animation should be drawn. In the example below, all of the shaded area will appear in view at some stage of the camera movement; the unshaded area will never appear in shot and therefore does not have to be drawn on. It is advisable, however, to draw the animation to a bleed line allowing the painted cels (including the backgrounds) to extend beyond the field edges. A bleed area of approximately half a field is sufficient.

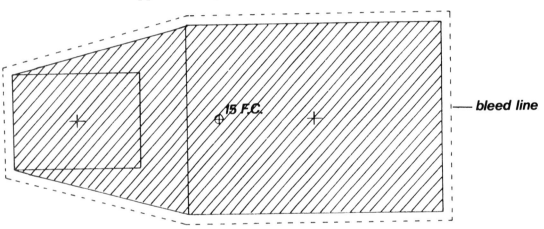

Occasionally, it is necessary for the animator to ask the cameraman to produce a pan that is on a curve or arc. In this case, it is necessary to draw on the field guide the required curved path of action of the centers of the fields. If, for example, the 4-field is moving to the 8-field on an upward curve, then the field guide and doping would appear as:

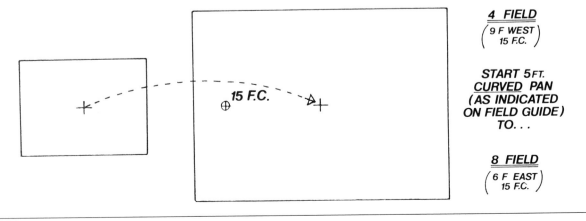

Panning Speeds

It is advisable for the animator to give the cameraman the center positions for each move on the pan, marked clearly on a path-of-action line on the field guide. The enlargement in the figure below indicates how this can be charted to guide the cameraman.

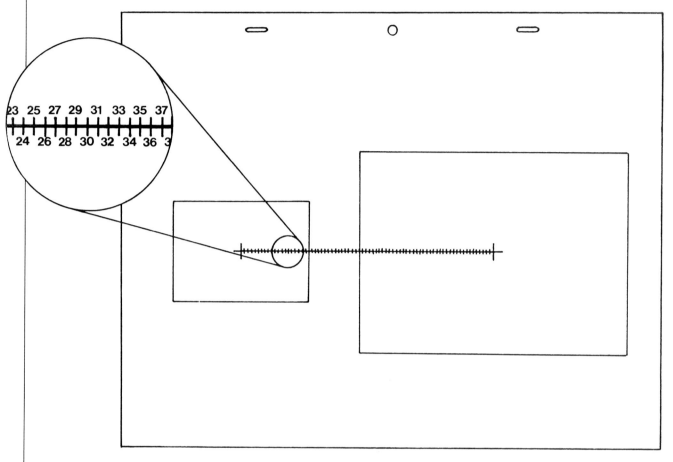

This is particularly important if the path of action of the pan is curved, or if the pan speed varies in any way, as in a slow-out or slow-in. In doing this, however, the animator must thoroughly understand panning speeds to avoid a strobing in the pan move. Remember that the slower the pan (that is, the less distance covered between moves), the smoother the pan, and the less chance of strobing. Although much is dependent on the nature of the visual images in the scene, a general rule to remember with pans is that anything greater than a move of 0.1 of an inch per frame move is likely to produce strobing. If, however, the camera is trucking in or out while it is panning, the outer edges of the field are likely to strobe, even if the center is moving to, or within, the 0.1-inch limit. This is because the outer edges of the field are moving further than the center movement. The center moves must then be slower to accommodate this.

When, on the other hand, the animation requires an extremely quick pan from one position to another—a zip pan—then it is possible to make the pan move extremely fast without incurring strobing. Subject to the nature of the scene, a general assumption is that moves of 0.25 of an inch or greater, will not create strobing problems.

If a zip pan is to be used, an effective way of adding drama to the action is—at the end of the pan—to travel just beyond the required end position, and then return to the hold at the end position in one, two, or three frames. This will give an excellent snap to the end of a frantic move. You should experiment with this and many other panning techniques in relation to the needs of the scene.

Camera shake, for example, creates the effect of the earth shaking if a character hits the ground from a great fall or runs into a wall after a speedy chase. The actual moves must be experimented with, but it is well to remember that the pans will jump from side to side of a center position and will lessen in distance as the effect of the crash diminishes and things become still.

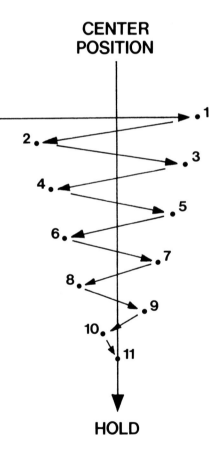

The golden rule of camera shakes is that the direction of the panning camera must be the same as the direction of the action causing the shake. In other words, if a character is running along a horizontal path and crashes into a vertical wall, the camera shake must be east-west. If, on the other hand, the character plummets down vertically and hits a horizontal object (such as the ground), then the camera shake must be north-south.

Assignment

Prepare a dope sheet and rework any of the tests you have previously done and are not happy with. Then draw the following field sizes:

A 12-field on a 15-field center

A 6-field on a 12-field center

Draw the following panning field guides:

A 6-field (6 F West/15 F.C.) to
a 6-field (6 F East/15 F.C.)

A 4-field (6 F South/12 F.C.) to
a 4-field (8 F North/12 F.C.)

Draw the following truck pan field guides:

A 4-field (8 F East/15 F.C.) to
an 8-field (11 F West/15 F.C.)

A 3-field (7 F North/12 F.C.) to
a 6-field (6 F South/12 F.C.) on an easterly curve

A 5-field (4 F North/8 F East/15 F.C.) to
an 8-field (5 F South/10 F West/15 F.C.)

EXAGGERATED ACTION

To emphasize a specific action or reaction, the animator can exaggerate the movement with a take, sneak, or stagger.

Takes and Double-Takes

In animation, the take is one of the most powerful ways to register surprise in a character. Simply defined, a take is an exaggerated reaction to an event. If, for example, a character is running along and suddenly his arch-enemy jumps out in front of him, his first reaction is that of shocked surprise—which is best underlined by his going into a take.

A take is an overreaction; therefore everything about it is over the top. The character's face, for instance, appears normal as he witnesses the event, but as a result of the event, it immediately goes into a squash. Then, from the squash, his face rises into a stretch, before returning to normal.

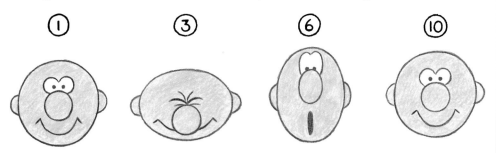

Animated on ones, the charting would be indicated as:

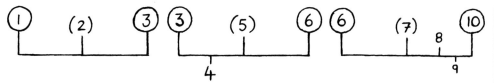

Alternatively, a profile take might appear:

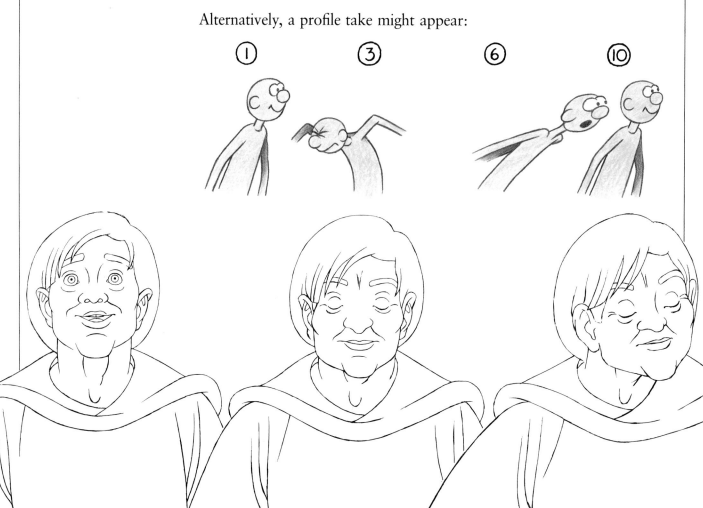

With a violent take, there is great anticipation in all the movements. If, for example, the head stretches up, it must first squash down. If the head stretches forward, it must first squash back.

An even more exaggerated take is the double-take. Quite simply, a double-take uses the same basic positions as the standard take, but has extreme and eccentric inbetweens. If the keys are:

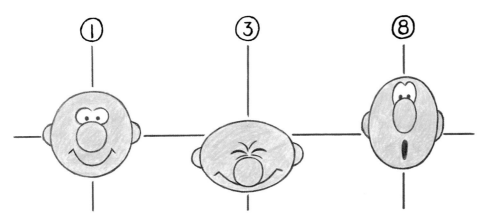

Then the inbetweens would be:

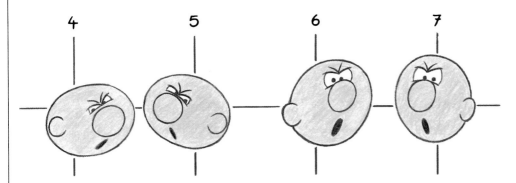

Note that the head swings violently from the left to right as it rises to the stretch position. The more extreme the action, the more violent the take will appear.

A full-body take is achieved in the same way as a facial take:

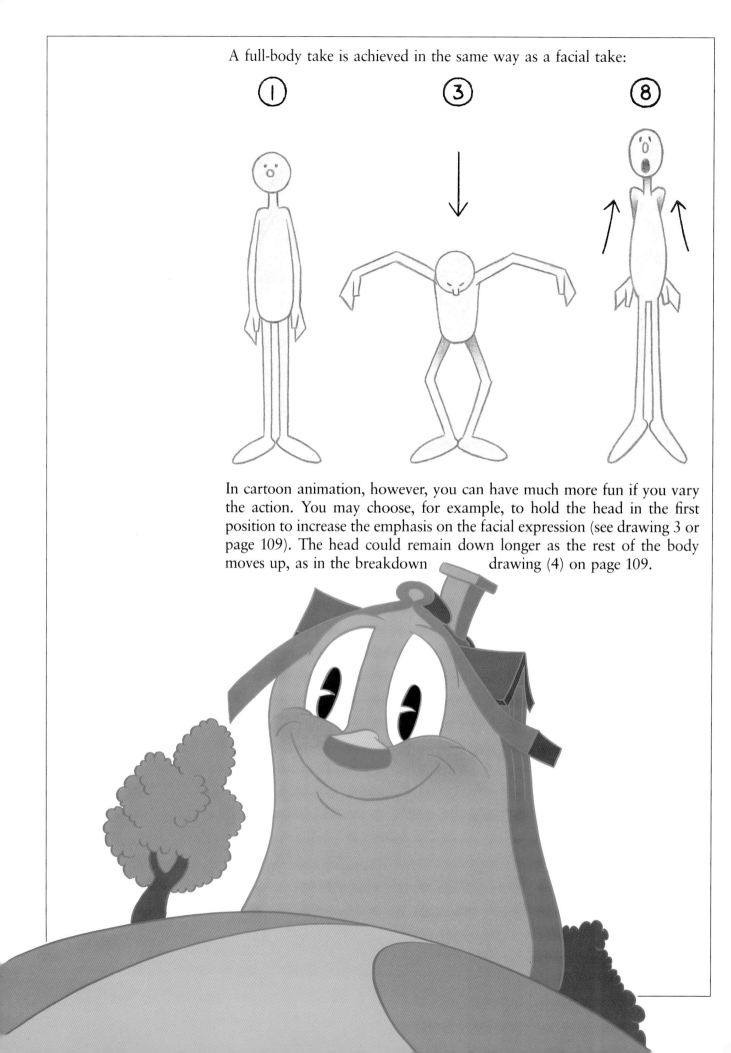

In cartoon animation, however, you can have much more fun if you vary the action. You may choose, for example, to hold the head in the first position to increase the emphasis on the facial expression (see drawing 3 or page 109). The head could remain down longer as the rest of the body moves up, as in the breakdown drawing (4) on page 109.

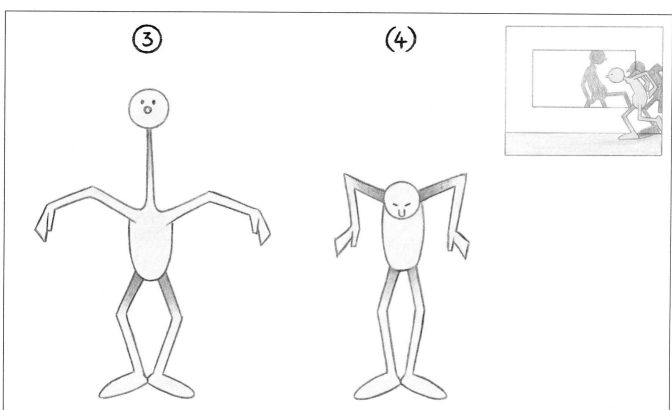

Alternatively, you might put a double-take on the head as it is rising. Indeed, with a take, anything can be thrown in to create the out-of-control effect that a violent reaction precipitates. In addition to squash and stretch, drag, distortion, and overlapping action are valuable tools when creating a believable and entertaining take. With drag, one part of the action is delayed—for example, when the Road Runner's head remains in the shot after his body has run out! With distortion, scale and proportion are exaggerated—for example, when a face moves close to the screen and is drawn exceptionally large to create a wide-angle lens effect. It is the ingenuity of the animator that separates one take from another.

Keep in mind, however, that stretch and squash are used in an extreme way only for cartoon characters. With flesh-and-bone, anatomical characters, there should be little visible stretch and squash; otherwise, the characters will look rubbery and unreal. To overcome this limitation, you can use exaggerated positioning, even when adhering to reality.

The sneak is another traditional animation technique for exaggerated action. Like walks, sneaks vary from character to character, and from animator to animator. The basic action of the sneak, however, falls into two distinct categories: the fast sneak and the slow sneak.

The fast sneak is what is often called the tippy-toe sneak. It is used when the character is moving fast, but trying to make as little noise as possible and not be noticed—for instance, when a character is rapidly sneaking up on a victim. There are a million examples of the fast sneak in the old Tom and Jerry cartoons. Basically, the fast sneak is characterized by the character's pose and the speed with which he moves. A typical fast-sneak pose is:

Note that the character is all hunched up (indeed, he is as compact as he can be, so that he can move unobserved). Also note that he only moves on the tips of his toes. The steps can be extremely fast and perky, with the character moving with a definite objective in mind. The average fast sneak is animated with anything up to 10 to 14 frames per step. There can be a great deal of up and down of the body during a fast sneak.

In contrast, the slow sneak is undertaken at a far more leisurely pace. It is usually used when a character is quietly trying to escape a situation—or rival—without being seen. The basic action of a slow sneak is much more forward and back than any other walk movement, but, again, the character remains on his toes to create a silent effect. The basic positions of a slow sneak are:

A suitable breakdown position might be:

Generally, a slow sneak is animated on at least 24 frames per step; the minimum, however, tends to be 16 frames per step. To obtain the necessary smoothness, it is advisable to animate the action on ones.

The backward sneak is an alternative to the slow sneak. It should be approached with much the same feeling and timing as the slow sneak, although the action has to be slightly modified.

It is important to stress that in every sneak the character is trying to move without being seen or heard. No matter what the animator attempts in terms of sophisticated movement, if the audience does not get this message, the action has failed.

After you have absorbed the basic principles of the sneak, try to inject some personality into the movement. The sneak of a tall, thin man, for example, will be different from that of a short, fat man. And a confident extrovert will move in a totally different manner from a nervous introvert. Interpretation is what separates top animators from the rest.

Staggers

Staggers contribute to the dynamics of the action. When, for example, an arrow hits a target, if it vibrates—or staggers—on impact, the effect of the hit is all the greater. Basically, staggers are more a doping technique than a drawing technique, although there can be exceptions. When an arrow hits the target (as on the left below), if it vibrates, the extremes of movement will be as shown on the right:

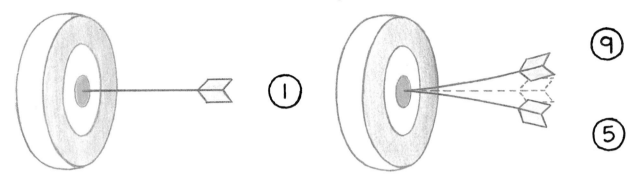

To get the desired stagger, you chart the inbetweens:

And dope them (on ones) thus:

⑤
⑨
4
8
(3)
(7)
2
6
①

This produces a decreasing displacement of the end of the arrow, until it reaches rest (drawing 1). For a smoother coming to rest, you could chart the inbetweens to give a slow-in from drawings 5 and 9.

① 3 (4) ⑤ AND ① 7 (8) ⑨
2 6

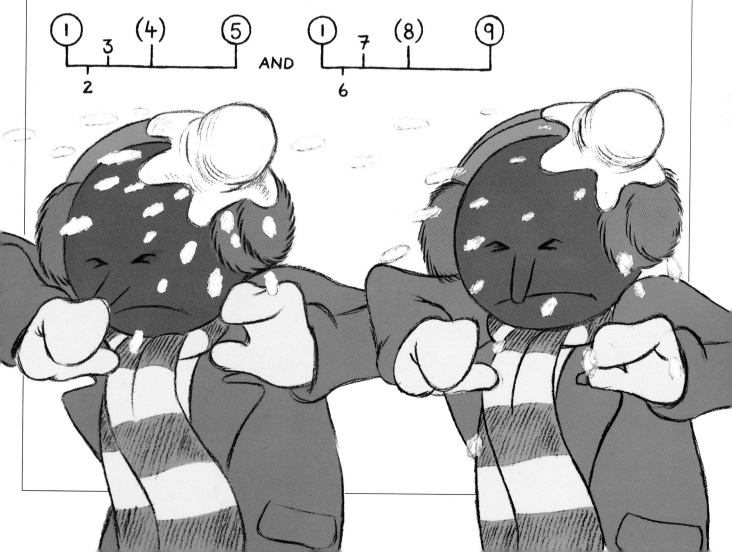

In a cartoon, a character may get hit by a heavy object and stagger, or vibrate, back to the rest position. This is handled in the same manner as the arrow.

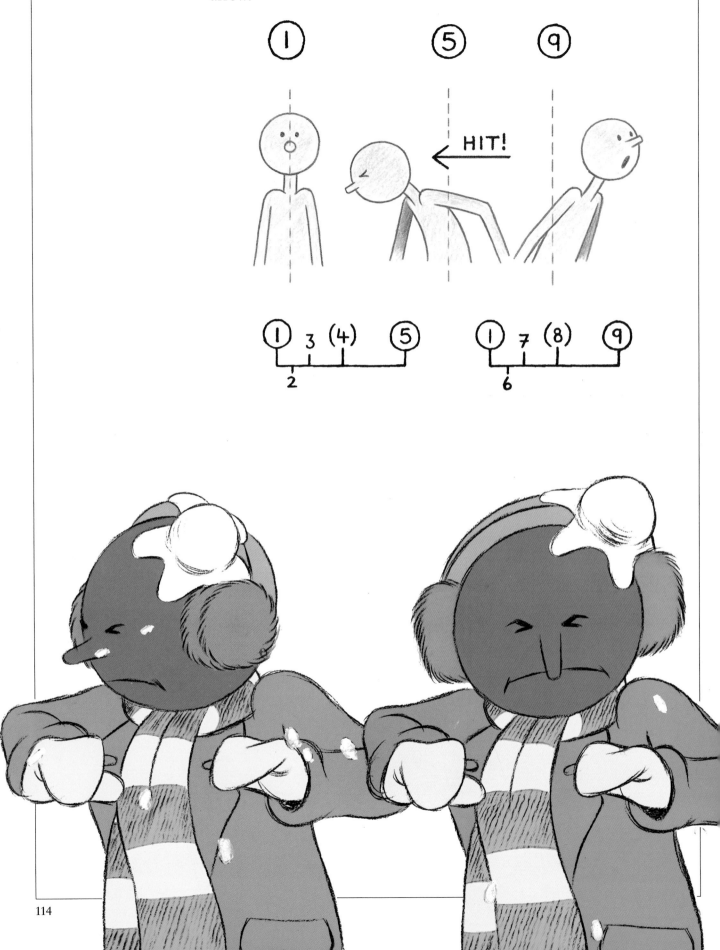

The doping might be:

For the greatest impact, the hit drawing 5 should immediately follow drawing 1, without inbetweens. Drawing 9—the reaction drawing—should not be displaced as far from the center position (drawing 1) as drawing 5. The number of inbetweens between the keys should be varied according to the requirements of the scene, as well as the strength and speed of the impact.

Staggers, when fully understood, can be used for a multitude of effects. It is not merely in dynamic action that the stagger can be used. Fear, for example, can be beautifully portrayed with stagger techniques.

At one time I had to animate a character nervously walking to the end of a diving board. Initially, I wanted to have his knees rapidly knocking together. I realized, however, that this would not show the tension in the springy diving board, so I devised an action—with staggers—which solved both problems. I began by animating the character walking along the board. The further he went along the board, the further it dipped.

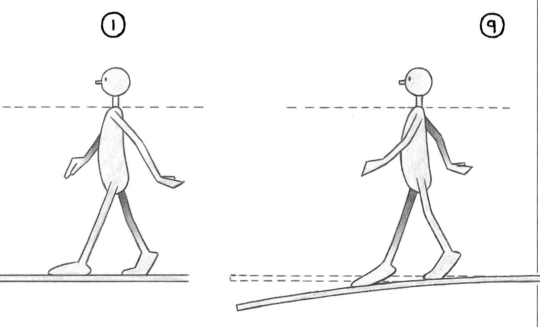

Then, I drew a second set of figures, identical to the first, except that, from the waist down, everything was animated as if the board had sprung back up slightly.

I charted the keys and doped them alternately.

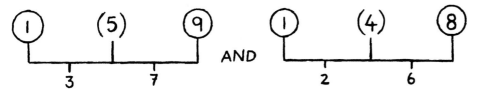 AND

$$
\begin{array}{c}
\textcircled{1} \\
\hline
2 \\
\hline
3 \\
\hline
(4) \\
\hline
(5) \\
\hline
6 \\
\hline
7 \\
\hline
\textcircled{8} \\
\hline
\textcircled{9}
\end{array}
$$

As a result, the upper body remained static throughout the walk, but the legs and the board vibrated underneath, giving the impression of mounting fear. The further along the board the character walked, the more the board bent, and the greater the buildup of tension because of the stagger.

An excellent example of stagger can be seen in the Roadrunner film in which the coyote swallows earthquake pills. There are a million and one ways that a stagger can be used—the only limitation is the animator's technique and imagination.

Assignment

Animate a sneak or a take of your choosing. If you have time, combine the two and have a real ball! Also animate an arrow hitting a target and staggering to a halt.

The Animal Kingdom

Animating birds and animals is an acquired art, requiring a great deal of careful study, although the basic movements can be broken down into simple formulas.

In animation there are traditionally four basic positions for a flying bird. The two most obvious are the wings-up and wings-down positions.

The breakdown positions, however, are not as straightforward. The traditional positionings of the breakdown drawings are:

Note the concave curve on the downward wing (2), as the wing tips drag against the air resistance of the downward thrust. When the wing reverses its direction upward again, there is a reversed curve, as the wing tips are dragged downward by the air resistance. These simple principles give a sense of flexibility and snap to the wings.

Although this simplified action is appropriate only for cartoon birds, the principle does apply in general terms to realistic flight patterns. Note the wing movements in the sequence of photographs by Eadweard Muybridge below (shown in profile and frontally). Position 6 represents the wings-up position, and position 3 the wings-down position. Both positions 1 and 2 could be described as breakdown positions on the downward flap, and you can see the concave curve made by the drag on the wing tips, particularly in position 2. In real life, however, the wings do not simply curve back the other way when they are on the way up, as they do in cartoon action. Instead, in real life, the structural anatomy of the wings must be taken into account. Observe the pronounced bend in the shape of the wings in position 4, which is really the breakdown position. Position 5, which constitutes the inbetween between 4 and 6, also has a bit of a convex curve, with the wing tips held down slightly. The shape of the wings then immediately reverses in position 6, as the movement begins to be directed down again.

Another important thing about bird flight is that due to the force of the wings against the air, the body is pushed slightly upward on the downward flap. Then, when the wings return upward again, the body drops slightly, resulting in a slight up-and-down movement of the bird's body as it flies along. With large, long-necked birds, such as swans and pelicans, there may also be an additional back-and-forth movement of the head, with the head and neck stretching on the downward flap and contracting when the wings are raised.

When animating bird flight, timing is essential for interpreting the size, personality, and nature of the bird. The dignity of an eagle in flight, for example, would be totally destroyed by the fast, jerky movements of a sparrow in flight. And the slow, powerful beats of the eagle's wings would be equally inappropriate for the sparrow. As a general rule, the larger the bird, the slower the action, and the smaller the bird, the faster the action. Also, the larger the wings, the more evident the up-and-down movement of the body will be. The smaller the wings, the less impact they will have on the body's movements.

It can be seen from Muybridge's photographs that the average pigeon flap is about six positions (shot on ones), but this must be varied according to the requirements of the scene. For a tiny bird, like a sparrow, a four-frame action might do.

The one exception to all of this is the hummingbird, whose wings move so fast that they cannot be captured by even one frame of film. In this case, the only way that the wing effect can be simulated is by using blurs. Instead of defining any wing shapes, the animator substitutes a blurred shape, which suggests the wing movements.

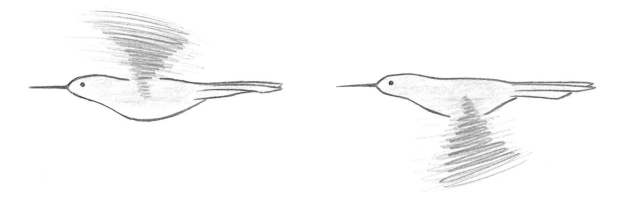

Generally, these blurs should be either above or below the horizontal center line, but they should vary considerably so that no repeatable pattern can be seen. If, for example, the hummingbird is hovering on the spot, as hummingbirds tend to do, then perhaps eight to twelve blurred overlays (half above, half below the center line) can be shot at random on ones. This will offer a great variety of alternative combinations of cels and will simulate the fast action of the wings. If you repeat drawings in this way, however, you must make sure that you re-dope each drawing at least four frames apart; otherwise, a flicker will occur, due to a kind of after-image and the idiosyncrasies of film optics. This blurring is best done with an airbrush or drybrush painting technique, rather than a drawn series of lines sketched in over the animation cel, which tends to look cheap and unattractive.

Butterflies

The blurred-wing technique is obviously ideal for the fast wing movements of all insects. For butterflies, however, a different technique can be used. Basically, the butterfly's wing movement can be achieved by two drawings, one with the wings up and the other with the wings down.

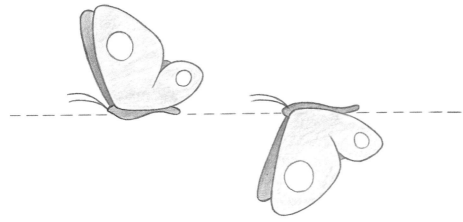

The animator can, of course, vary the amount of up and down from drawing to drawing. Indeed, a butterfly's action is distinguished by its erratic flight path. Butterflies appear to flit and dance all over the place, although they usually seem to be headed in one general direction. The golden rule when animating butterflies is that—because of the extreme lightness of their bodies—whenever the wings flap down, the body moves up dramatically, and whenever the wings flap up, the body moves down dramatically.

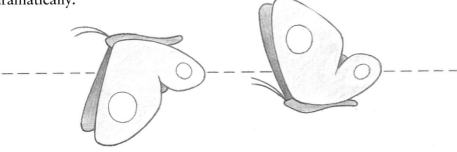

The degree of up and down of the body is decided by the individual animator, although it should be as irregular as possible and not at all repetitive. Indeed, the best way to animate butterflies is to sketch out a general path of action, then draw in, straight ahead, each consecutive drawing, judging the movement intuitively. In other words, you do not use keys and inbetweens, but animate one drawing directly after another.

Human walks are difficult enough, but when you double the number of legs, you double the problems. If, however, four-legged walks are approached from the cartoon point of view, then the solution becomes clearer—as long as the basic principles of standard human walks have already been mastered. Basically, the walk of the cartoon horse can be divided into two independent human walks, one for the front legs (A) and one for the back legs (B).

To get the horse to move, first animate the front legs (A) as in the human walk, at the speed and in the manner you want them to go. Then repeat the same thing with the back legs (B). Make sure, however, that the ground covered by the back legs is the same as that covered by the front legs; otherwise, the body will seem to stretch apart, or fold up like an accordion (which might be amusing, if done consciously). All the rules about up-and-down movement of the body apply, of course.

When walking four legs together, it is also necessary to ascertain how the action of the front legs will synchronize with the action of the back legs. A brief look at Muybridge's photographs of a moving horse shows that,

essentially, when the front right leg is forward, the back right leg is back (position 1) and when the front right leg is back, the back right leg is forward. Of course, this is an oversimplification of what is going on, but, for cartoon purposes, it is a good starting point.

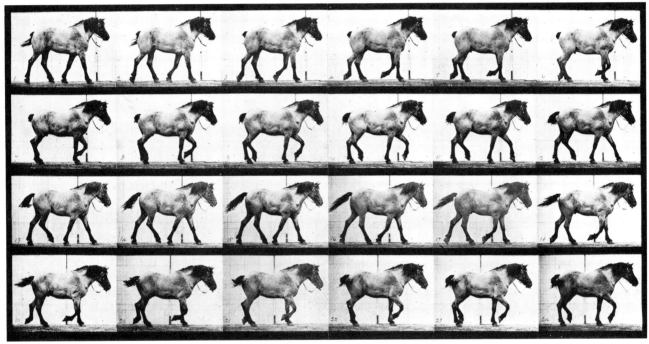

Rules, however, are made to be broken, and the funniest cartoon walks can be achieved by totally disregarding the rules. What if the back right leg moves forward at the same time as the front right leg?

Or if the front legs move normally but the back legs have a double-bounce?

The variations are endless. In cartoon four-legged walks, as with all animation, it is the animator's imagination that makes the action work successfully. With the great variation of up-and-down movements and leg actions available in walks, there should be every opportunity to come up with something totally original for a four-legged walk.

After the legs and linking body are completed, it is a simple matter to add the head and tail. The head and neck will react to the general action of the front legs, so normally you might expect to see the head move up as the shoulders move down, and down as the shoulders move up again. In the same way, the tail tends to flick down as the haunches move up, and up as the haunches go down. But since rules are made to be broken, you can and should use your imagination to bring some originality into the action.

When, however, we move out of the realm of cartoon four-legged walks, and into the realistic world, the problems are accentuated. A careful study of the way the animal moves must be made because absolute authenticity is demanded. *Animals in Motion*, Eadweard Muybridge's book of sequenced photographs, is an invaluable source of reference material and a must for all animators who care enough to get the most out of their craft. A study of the sequence illustrated above will reveal a great deal about timing and action in relation to the walking horse. But, however complicated the action appears, all the principles of movement previously explained still apply.

As Art Babbit, the great ex-Disney animator, once said, all the animator has to do is "observe, analyze, file it, and interpret it." When interpreting real-life action, however, it is necessary to caricature it to some extent, by exaggerating the observed action. This is the reason that, when live-action film is simply traced (rotascoped) and then put on animation cel and shot, the action is dull and wooden. (Critics of modern animation directors will appreciate this point.) It is only by caricaturing the movement, and applying all the principles previously explained, that the action will come alive. Anything else is cheating and does little service to the fine tradition of drawn animation.

Tips on Animating Animals

The characteristics of animals, like the personalities of humans, vary so much that no simple formulas can be given. Is the animal heavy or light? Is it slow and laborious, or jumpy and nervous? Is it carrying a weight on its back, or is it free of restriction? Such variables as these are important to think about before you begin animating the movement. Your own observation and analysis will teach you how to achieve a particular objective.

A few simple tips, however, may prove useful.

☐ Heavy waterbirds tend to need a run before they can take off for flight.

☐ Large birds tend to glide in the air a lot and usually need only a minimum of flaps to remain airborne once they have achieved altitude.

☐ When an animal is leaping, there is a curved line to the body as the animal strides and lands.

☐ When animating a horse, or any other animal, realistically, it is helpful to rough out the action in simple boxes representing the main body mass. After the space and action for this are achieved, the legs, and then the head and tail, can be drawn. This is best drawn lightly and roughly until the action is acceptable; it can be cleaned up afterward.

☐ Small rodents, like mice, do not generally need much up-and-down body movement. It is a simple procedure to animate the body moving fast across the scene in a fairly straight line, adding scurrying afterward to complete the effect.

☐ Snakes tend to slither along a wavy path of action, with little or no body action.

☐ For the bounce of a kangaroo, use the bouncing-ball principle. Contact with the ground should be kept to a minimum, with the greatest emphasis on the slow-in and slow-out drawings at the height of the bounce.

☐ On all cat springs there should be a slow windup before the spring (anticipation), a sudden spring, and a slight slow-in at the top of the leap. (Keep in mind the sprinter's start on page 70.)

Assignment

Animate either an eagle chasing a pigeon or a horse approaching and clearing a fence. Do not clean up your drawings; rough drawings will do.

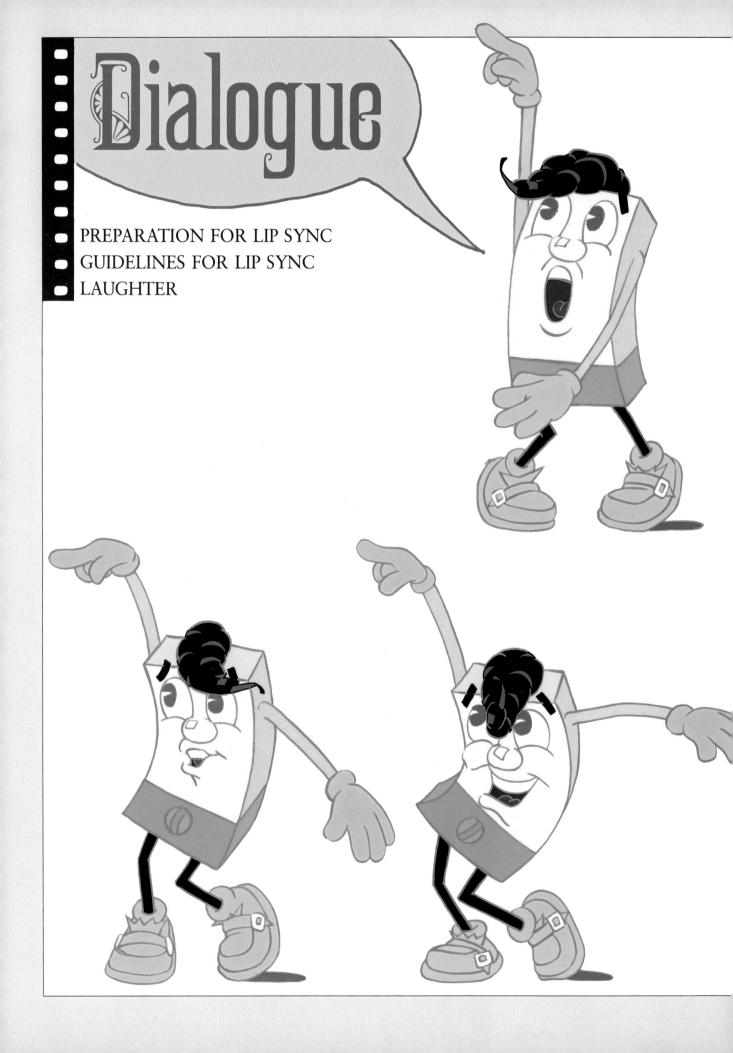

Dialogue

PREPARATION FOR LIP SYNC
GUIDELINES FOR LIP SYNC
LAUGHTER

Accurate lip sync is essential if animation incorporating dialogue is to appear convincing and natural.

We take lip sync for granted in live-action film—and, indeed, in life—but when it has to be simulated in moving drawings, problems arise. Accurate observation and analysis of what is happening when words are spoken will make the task easier.

For perfect choreography between the recorded word and the animated picture, a number of important stages have to be undertaken with great precision and care. First, the sound editor has to analyze the recorded voice and make a phonetic breakdown. To achieve a phonetic breakdown, the editor basically runs a 35mm magnetic track (if the film is 35mm) over an editing sound head and identifies, frame by frame, the particular sound, or part of a word, which is being spoken on the track at any particular frame. Then, frame by frame, the editor writes on the nonmagnetic side of the track a phonetic interpretation of what is heard.

Obviously, it is essential that the editor be accurate and conscientious; otherwise, whatever error is made at this stage will continue to appear throughout the remaining operation. Corrections made later entail redrawing, at great expense of time and money.

Having broken down the soundtrack, the editor then transfers all the markings to a bar sheet, which is a visual representation of the soundtrack. Starting from frame 1, the editor marks the relevant frames on the bar sheet with the identical phonetic markings used on the 35mm magnetic track. The bar sheet then appears as:

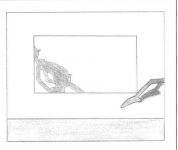

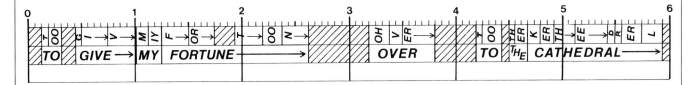

When the bar sheet is complete, the animator can take over. Using the bar sheet and a fresh dope sheet, the animator transposes all the information, frame by frame, from the bar sheet to the dialogue column of the dope sheet.

Now all the technical procedures are completed and the animator can begin to be creative. It is always wise, however, to first write the column of animation drawing numbers on the dope sheet so that the relevant accent drawings can be identified before any key drawings are attempted.

SEQUENCE ①	SCENE ①	DIALOGUE TEST						SHEET ①
		5	4	3	2	1	B G	CAMERA INSTRUCTIONS
	▨				1			
	T OO				3			START
					5			
	▨				7			
	G				9			
	↓				11			
	↓				13			
	V				15			
①	↓				17			
	M				19			
	IY				21			
	F				23			
	↓				25			
	OR				27			
	↓				29			
	▨				31			
②	T				33			

Accents are extremely important to the lip-sync process. If you observe an actor or TV announcer speaking, you will note that certain parts of each statement are accented by head, hand, or body movements, as if to underline their importance. Similarly, a politician who wants to appear authoritative or sincere about a certain point will accent a particular word or phrase with a definite head or hand movement, often thumping the podium with sincerity. Accents, therefore, are essential to making any emphasis in speech convincing. The recorded track itself will suggest where the accents should occur, so a repeated playing, over and over again, of the track is necessary before the animator can commit visual ideas to paper. The animator should therefore ask for a cassette tape of the soundtrack when ordering the bar sheet from the editor. The animator should also make sure that if the character is supposed to be singing, the editor has indicated on the bar sheet where all the main beats occur in the music (as well as the identifiable instrumentation, if necessary), since these are invariably important accent points in the action.

The Disney animators discovered that accents in lip-sync dialogue always worked best if they were placed approximately three to four frames ahead of the actual sync point to be accented. If, for example, a character were to sneeze, the picture would show the sneeze action three or four frames ahead of the actual sneeze sound. The animators found no logical reason for this. But since it worked, they made it a general rule. Sometimes they would even put an accent 12 or 16 frames ahead of the sound, depending on the nature of the sound to be accented.

For the sneeze, then, the dialogue column of the dope sheet might be marked like this:

More generally, with lip-sync dialogue, the animator first marks the dope sheet with all the accent points suggested by the repeated playing of the soundtrack to be animated. Then the animator circles the corresponding numbers for the animation drawings to establish the key drawings.

SEQUENCE ①		SCENE ①		DIALOGUE TEST					
			5	4	3	2	1	B G	
						1			
		T OO				3			
						5			
SQUASH ⊕						7			
		G				9			
						11			
		V				13			
						15			
①		M				17			
		IY				19			
UP ⊕		F				21			
						23			
		OR				25			
						27			
						29			
						31			
②		T				33			

After the key drawings are animated, the animator will probably draw the breakdown drawings before handing the scene on to the assistant for inbetweening. To avoid confusion, the animator should ask the assistant not to draw in the mouths and chins on the inbetweens. Instead, the animator should do these when the lip sync on the inbetween is ready to be completed.

Lip sync is an art in itself, and not all animators have an aptitude for it. A few gifted animators have a real feel for the interpretation of dialogue, but most animators must work hard just to make it work adequately.

Acceptable lip sync can be achieved by remembering a few important guidelines:

☐ All mouth positions should correspond to the frame of the sound indicated in the dialogue column. Animators sometimes suggest that the lip sync can be drawn one or two frames ahead of the dialogue, and this can also be successful. If, however, the lip sync is all drawn level-sync, it makes it easier for the editor to move the picture backward or forward in relation to the track, if the need arises. The lip sync should never be drawn behind sync—that is with the picture appearing after the sound is heard—unless there is a special reason for doing so.

☐ If the dialogue is so fast that the changing phonetic sounds occur every frame, then the animation has to be put on ones instead of twos. If this is difficult, it may be possible to leave the mouth drawings off the main animation drawings and place them on an overlay cel. In this way, the mouth animation could be on ones while the head and body animation remained on twos, although this is often not as desirable as having everything drawn on ones.

☐ With lip sync, it is essential to emphasize strongly all the vowel sounds—*a*, *e*, *i*, *o*, *u*—while the consonants can, to some extent, be treated as less important. This emphasis is achieved by immediately banging open the mouth for all vowel sounds and then returning to natural movements for the consonants. If the vowel sound is prolonged, then the maximum open position should, in most cases, be achieved on the first frame of the sound. The mouth should then be slowly inbetweened to a slightly more closed position, although remaining emphatically open. (This is known as a moving hold.) Sometimes, a vowel sound accent can be drawn one frame ahead of level-sync animation.

Obviously, the soundtrack will dictate which vowel sounds are most important but, as a general rule, the mouth-open sounds tend to dominate the action. If the open positions hit their sounds accurately, then the lip sync is usually successful. Theoretically, then, it should be possible to suc-

cessfully lip-sync any foreign language, even if you do not understand it—provided all the principal vowel sounds are correctly indicated and you pay proper attention to the accents of the track.

☐ Certain consonants, however, are important when tackling lip sync. In particular, *b*, *f*, *m*, and *l* should, ideally, be held for at least two frames.

☐ The shape of the mouth in dialogue can vary considerably from character to character. If the same soundtrack were visualized for a tight-lipped, heavy character and a wide-mouthed, thin character, the results would look very different. As with everything else in animation, you must first feel the personality of the character and its limitations of expression and form.

☐ It is absolutely necessary to have a mirror in front of you and to act out the dialogue for yourself, before putting pencil to paper. It is only by observation from life that you really begin to understand movement. Since it is not possible for you to have the voice actor with you at your lightbox, you yourself must become the animated character and act the dialogue action in the mirror. The satisfaction of producing a successful dialogue action should far outweigh any self-consciousness or inhibition you may feel about acting like a fool in front of a mirror. It is only by seeing the shape and movement of your own mouth that you can begin to understand how the animated character's mouth will perform.

☐ Unless the character is a loud, wild person, most lip sync can be underplayed, except for important accents and vowel sounds. This is especially true in realistic characterizations, where the barest minimum of mouth movement can be successful. Indeed, much lip-sync animation is spoiled, not by an inaccurate interpretation of the mouth movements involved, but by an overemphasis of the actual movements. For more discrete animation, always hit the vowels and accents strongly, but let the changes in the shape of the mouth flow smoothly, subtly, and naturally.

☐ In closeups of dialogue, the audience always watches the eyes, so the accents and emphasis must always be initiated in the eyes, before the rest of the face and mouth is even considered. In long shots, do not forget the importance of the whole body in applying accents and emphasis.

☐ Up-and-down movements and subtle left-to-right tilts of the head are another important way of emphasizing dialogue and giving life to the character.

Animating laughter successfully is difficult but important. The manner in which a character moves when laughing will vary as much as laughs vary. But there are two basic formulas that will help in simplistic animation.

The simplest laugh, and therefore the one to be avoided by all self-respecting animators, is the stagger laugh. This laugh is simply a straightforward inbetweening of two key drawings:

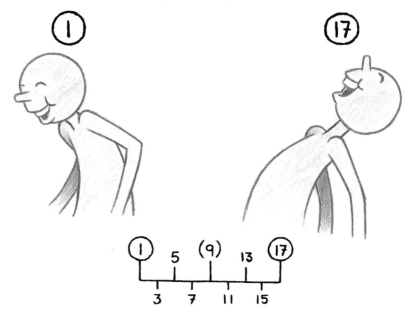

But it is doped like a stagger action, thereby producing a simple shaking movement.

①
3
5
3
7
5
(9)
7
11
(9)
13
11
15
13
⑰
15
⑰

A slightly more sophisticated variation of the stagger laugh occurs when overlapping action is added to the movement. If, for example, the shoulders rise as the head sinks and the head rises as the shoulders sink, the effect begins to be more convincing. One way to do this is to have two sets of keys. In one the head is down and the shoulders are up:

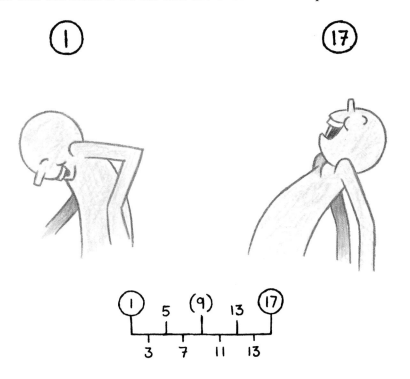

In the other, the head is up and the shoulders are down.

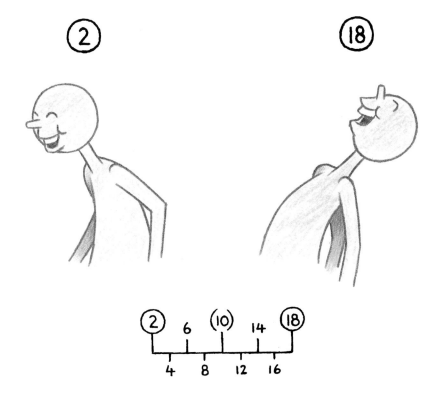

These two sets can then be inter-doped on ones or twos, producing another variation of the laugh.

①
②
3
4
5
6
7
8
(9)
(10)
11
12
13
14
15
16
⑰
⑱

Whatever the type of laugh, it is best animated straight ahead, with no keys, in strict accordance with the accents on the phonetic breakdown. Since a laugh is an uncoordinated emotional outburst, it is always uncoordinated in its movement. Take full advantage of this opportunity and allow your inventiveness to be limited only by the track requirements.

When animating a laugh or any other dynamic action, it may be helpful to throw in an extra key drawing (on a one) immediately after what might be considered the final extreme key drawing. If, for instance, the character has reached the top key of a sudden laugh movement (number 17) and is about to return to a normal position, you could throw in an extra extreme drawing (number 18) immediately before the first downward inbetween, thereby adding impact to the movement.

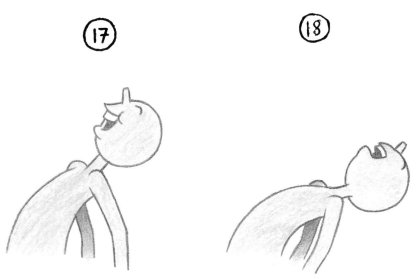

The result, although virtually subliminal, is extremely effective. Keep in mind, however, that this technique works only for sudden, fast, chaotic, or uncoordinated movements, such as laughs, shocks, and takes.

Assignment

First, create a track breakdown from a soundtrack of your choice, or try to obtain an existing track breakdown from an animation editor. Then, animate a simple talking head (a ball with eyes and mouth will do) in perfect synchronization to the chosen track. Use as much invention as possible to accent the words, but remember that the audience's judgment of successful dialogue animation is always based on the natural interpretation and believability of the dialogue movements.

ANIMATED EFFECTS

WIND
WATER
FIRE
SOLID OBJECTS

Animated effects (SF/X) can add realism, drama, and atmosphere to animation, and are thus an important skill to master.

It is difficult to indicate wind unless you have such obvious props as flags or laundry on a line, which are affected by the wind's movement. An animated character, however, can also be affected by the wind. If, for example, a man is walking into the wind, then the stronger the wind, the more he must appear to lean into it to make progress.

Props can be added to emphasize the power of the wind. If the man is wearing a hat and a long raincoat, they will be affected by the wind. As the man walks, he will have to hold the hat on his head, and the hat may even be carried off by the wind to emphasize its speed and direction. The coat will be pushed back and will flap if the wind is particularly strong.

The flapping movement of any loose material caught in the wind is best shown in the animation of a flag. When the wind is not blowing, the flag hangs limply. But when the wind blows gently, the flag bellows out slightly. And if the wind is really strong, the flag is pushed straight out.

Always let the flag fall to rest occasionally, because a gust of wind usually dies down before the next one arrives. Variation and lack of consistency are

the key things to remember when animating wind. This should be reflected in your animation, whether it is a flag or the coat on a walking figure.

Another effect that might be worth trying when animating wind is to draw a number of vertical lines across the screen, each set on a separate cel, of course.

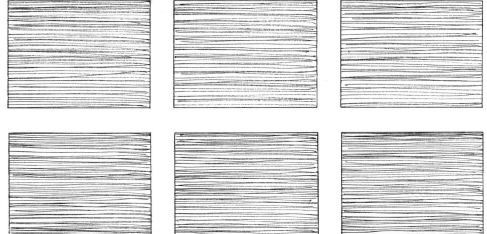

These can then be doped at random, so there is no repetitive pattern. If the cels are shot at less than 100 percent exposure over the scene, they will be seen just enough to give an erratic sense of direction to the wind. To obtain the right exposure, direct the cameraman to shoot a wedge test of the effects artwork over the background—that is, ask for the effects artwork to be shot at varying exposures from 0 to 100 percent on separate frames of film. You might, for example, request that the exposures rise by 10 percent on each frame (from 10 to 20 to 30 percent, and so on). From this test, the best frame of film can be selected and the final exposure of the animated effects can be determined.

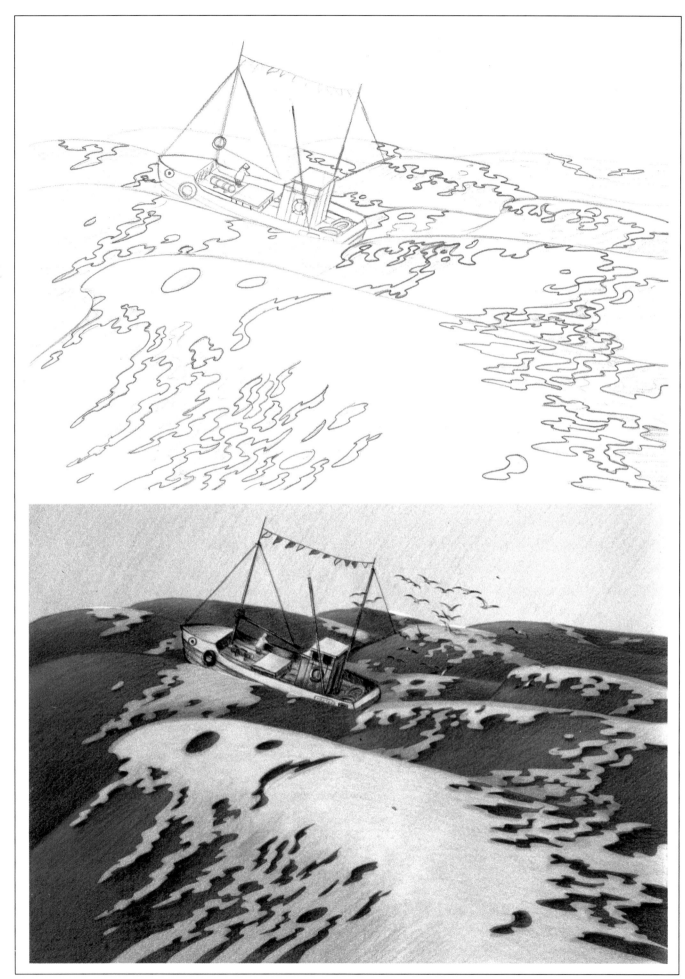

Filming animated effects at less than 100 percent exposure is a technique that is frequently used to simulate effects in real life. This is particularly true when you are animating flowing water. On a simple level, the effect of flowing water can be created by first establishing a plain background color for the water and then animating a series of shapes across it to simulate the feeling of movement you get when you watch a running stream. The shapes can be abstract, stylized, or realistic.

 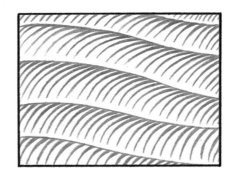

Whatever shapes you select, they should flow in a consistent way, following the chosen path of action. They can be repeated on a cycle if you are restricted in time and budget, but because water action, like wind, is never mechanical, it is advisable to produce a number of cycles and repeat them at random so that there is no observable repetition. Once animated, these drawings should be colored in a darker shade of the background color and, perhaps, shot at less than 100 percent exposure.

If the water action is more violent than a simple flowing movement, you can add another level of animation, depicting whitecaps at the top of the waves.

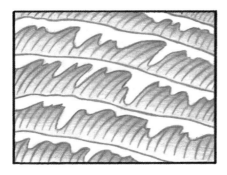

The whitecaps are best placed on another cel level. Then, if you are using cycle animation for the wave effects, you can at least vary the whitecaps (preferably animating them straight ahead) to avoid similarity and repetitiveness. Drawing the whitecaps on a separate level will also give you the opportunity to experiment with the percentage of the exposure, since 100 percent white might be too strong.

These basic techniques are applicable when animating all flowing water, including waterfalls, running taps, and moving streams and rivers. Of course, the techniques must be developed according to the demands of the scene.

Another simple, but extremely effective technique can be used to show shimmering sunlight or moonlight on the surface of a lake, river, or sea. Basically, all that is necessary is a series of cels with varied interpretations in white of the reflected light.

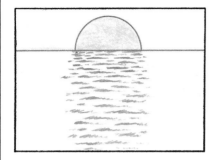 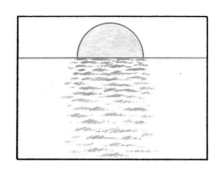 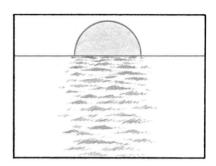

After the cels are completed, the animator merely dissolves from one to the other, at random, on simple mixes from two frames per mix to ten frames, depending on the speed of the effect required. This produces a beautiful, changing pattern of reflected light on the surface of the water. Greater sophistication can be achieved by having two cel levels at the same time—one mixing, perhaps, on four frames per mix, while the other might be eight frames per mix. This gives a constantly changing image in which the regularity of the mixes is more difficult to detect.

The same technique can be used to indicate the moving surface of a lake or sea, when a random effect of small moving waves is desired. Several cels—the more, the better—are drawn in black or colored line in the required style:

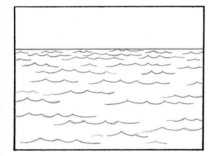 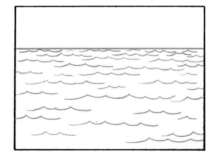 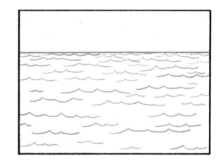

Then they are mixed one to another, at random, at the required speed. This technique can be highly successful even with a minimum of cells.

Reflections can be achieved by reversing the animation to be reflected so it is upside down and shooting it at a percentage exposure in the required position. A character might, for example, be walking along a river bank on top pegs.

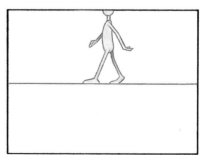

It would be quite possible to trace, upside down, the identical action on a separate cel and then shoot it at less than 100 percent exposure.

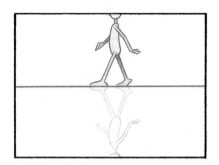

Unfortunately, this method can be used only when the surface on which the reflection is to appear is perfectly smooth. If the water is moving or rippling, the reflected image should become distorted in proportion to the amount of disturbance present. The rougher the water, the greater the breakup of the image.

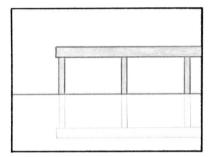 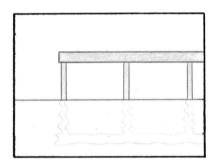 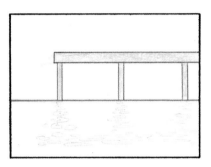

Rain can be treated similarly to wind. On live-action film, rain is seen, frame by frame, more as a blur than as a mass of droplets, so it is best to try to produce a series of cels that simulate this effect. Use a series of cels with grayish diagonal lines (or lines at a percentage of black) and then dope them at random to produce a rain effect.

 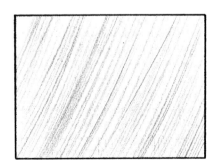 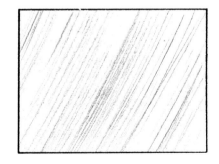

This effect is enhanced if the rain cels appear on more than one level and each level is a slightly different color and texture. The impact is further increased if the background behind a particularly heavy rain is subdued and seems out of focus.

Fire is most effective if a backlighting camera effect is attempted. Fire is luminous and needs the added bite of the glow that backlighting produces, rather than the dead look of painted flames.

The simplest fire effect is that of a candle flame. A candle flame moves very little, unless it is fanned by a draft from an open door or window, so it can be quickly produced. Basically, there need be only three key positions of the flame, each moving only a little from the others.

There can then be several inbetweens to produce a slow, almost imperceptible, movement. When completed, these drawings should be traced in negative on acetate, so they are clear against a black surround.

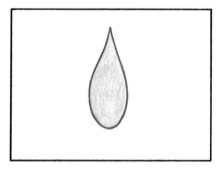 

ORIGINAL DRAWING   PAINTED CEL

The cameraman can then shine a strong, diffused light from behind, through the clear part of the cel, and produce a wedge test of the light's intensity. Having chosen a satisfactory exposure from the wedge test, the cameraman then shoots the finished scene, first filming everything in the scene except the candle flame, and then running the film back in the camera and shooting the flame animation effect at the desired exposure. For added effectiveness, the candle flame can be shot either out of focus or with a fog filter over the camera lens to give a softness to the flame. A slightly yellow filter can be added to the backlighting to kill the harsh whiteness, which might be overpowering.

A raging fire requires the same camera techniques, but, of course, the animation must be more dynamic. A fire flickers erratically, and the animation should reflect this.

To achieve the most startling effects, it is best to animate a fire on several cel levels, with each level having a slightly different color intensity. The buildup and overlay of these levels will give the fire life and depth.

A common fault in fire animation is that no allowance is made for the effect of the fire on the rest of the scene. If you observe a real fire, you will see that the firelight flickers over the objects in the scene and that shadows are cast by all the solid objects. To achieve the flicker of firelight, it is necessary to produce a number of varying airbrushed cels, which slightly heighten the surfaces on the background of the scene. When these are doped at random throughout the scene, they create a flickering effect throughout.

Shadows are a little more complicated to create. If a character stands in the sun, a shadow will be cast along the ground as well as along the side of the character farthest away from the sun.

When animating shadows, therefore, it is first necessary to work out the direction of the light source. Then, drawing by drawing, you must meticulously indicate those parts of the character which are shielded from the light and the shape of the shadow the character creates on the ground. These drawings are then transferred to a separate cel level, different from that at which the animation is shot, and filmed at a percentage exposure less than the rest of the scene (using a wedge test to ascertain the percentage needed). This produces a translucent, yet darkening, effect. The shadows are usually painted black on the cel, but they can be other dark shades, perhaps brown or blue, to reflect the color mood of the scene.

Solid objects are so diverse that it is difficult to pin them down to any one formula. It must be left to the animator's ingenuity to solve any challenging problems that arise. Several tips can be offered, however, for some of the most frequently encountered problems.

A common difficulty occurs when an object in a highly rendered background begins to move. How, for example, can a realistic boulder be moved from its place in the background? If it is animated with flat cel paint at the moment it begins to move, the change in texture is easily noticed. There are two ways around this—one easy, the other difficult.

The easy way is to paint the boulder separately from the background on a cutout, and lightly stick it down in its appropriate position. Then the boulder can simply be moved a little at a time—in relation to the animation action compelling the move—until it comes to rest once more, or leaves the scene. This can be successful in some scenes, but usually it is unsatisfactory because the boulder continues to look like a two-dimensional cutout, while the rest of the scene is animated in a more three-dimensional way.

The harder, but more effective, procedure is to animate the boulder in a more three-dimensional way to fit in with the rest of the animation and then to render each animation drawing so that it looks precisely like the background style. This may entail a whole series of painted, airbrushed, or pencil-shaded boulder drawings—each matching perfectly the animation shapes and movements created by the animator, yet at the same time appearing identical in color and texture to the style of the background. Obviously, this rendering technique is extremely time- and money-consuming, but visually it can produce remarkable effects.

Another problem, which occurs principally in advertising, is when a number of products with special package designs have to be moved in a scene. A character may be holding a bottle that has an intricately designed

label. To avoid the tedious, repetitious drawing of hundreds of perfect labels (on which, of course, most advertisers insist) it is possible to plan the scene so the animator has to use only one. This, it must be stressed, can be done only if the bottle remains the same size throughout the action. (If the bottle changes size or perspective, then the numerous changing labels have to be drawn by hand.) The bottle is simply animated with everything but the label design showing. Then all that is required is an accurate tracing, on each drawing, of the label outline, which remains in the same place in relation to the rest of the bottle on every drawing. When the drawings are painted, the bottle is colored as usual, but the area within the label outline is left clear. Then a beautifully produced piece of label artwork is drawn and cut out to perfectly match the label outline drawn on each of the bottle cels. When shooting, the cameraman places the label artwork behind the clear space on each bottle cel, so that the label appears to be the same on every bottle. This technique, of course, can be used for the whole bottle—and not just the label—using a drawn bottle outline as the animation guide.

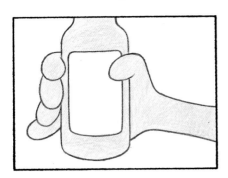

Effects animation is an art form in itself, and when it is successfully produced it can add the magic so often lacking in animation. Unsuccessfully produced, however, it can hinder and distract from the animator's work. Therefore, always pay careful attention to the effects techniques under consideration.

BACKGROUNDS

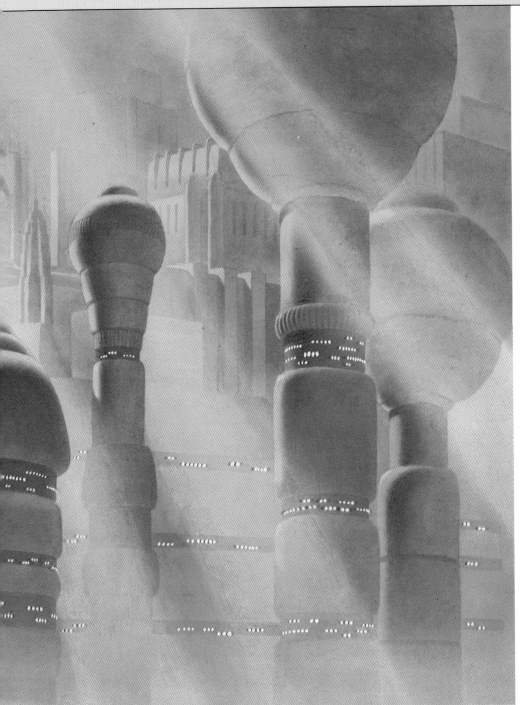

Backgrounds are critical to the effectiveness of the end product in animation and should never be neglected or undervalued.

Often the background fills more than 90 percent of the scene. Because it is static for the duration of each scene, it has to stand up to close scrutiny, particularly on a large motion-picture screen. Indeed, the whole mood of a film can be either enhanced or destroyed by the quality of the background art. Obviously, it pays to spend time and effort on backgrounds.

It has long been my opinion that the skill of the better background artists far exceeds that of many highly respected book illustrators. Even a cursory glance at the background art reproduced here should show this. But illustrative expertise alone is not enough when it comes to producing background artwork for film. The background artist must be precise and accurate in executing the artwork since much of the animation in a scene is created to precisely match a particular registration point, or matchline, in the background design. If the background artist fails to account for this in the artwork, it may lead to disaster when the animation and background are combined. When matchline positions are indicated in the background layout, the background artist has to reproduce them exactly in the artwork. If no matchlines are indicated, the background artist has more license in interpreting the layout design. (The background art has to conform to the same peg registration system used for the animation. Often this means that registration peg holes of the appropriate size must be carefully and accurately hand-cut with a craft knife.)

The background artist should be given clear instructions by the director or designer about the mood and action of the particular scene. It is impor-

tant to know, for example, whether the color relates directly to the preceding or following scene. Constantly bearing the overall mood in mind, the background artist has to choose colors and coloring techniques to conform to the demands of the scene, and decide whether the colors should be strongly applied or toned down for more subtle effects.

A common mistake of background artists is to put too much texture into the colors they paint, which can conflict with the flat colors of the animation itself. Nothing is more disconcerting for a viewer than to instantly become aware of a disparity between these two elements in a scene. Obviously, the background artist must take care to avoid this.

Although many mediums can be selected for the background treatment, if a watercolor approach is contemplated, the artist must stretch the background paper before the layout design is transferred to the surface for coloring. If this is not done, the paper may expand after watercolor is applied to it, and distortion or inaccuracy may creep into any matchlines that are indicated. Moreover, if water-based paints are used on unstretched paper, the paper will cockle. Such cockling is a headache for the rostrum cameraman, who has to make sure that every part of the background artwork lies flat on the tabletop under the camera to avoid shadowing from the animation cels (which always happens under camera lights when the cel is not in full contact with the background beneath it). Although the rostrum pressure glass and a light padding of tissue paper behind the artwork may eliminate this problem to some extent, it is in the best interest of the film that the background artist avoid this situation in the first place by stretching the paper.

The background artwork reproduced here suggests the range and sophistication of artwork that can be used in animated films. Such artwork requires time and money to produce, and unfortunately there is a current trend—worldwide—to lower production values and reduce budgets. The discriminating animator, however, should always try to pursue the highest standards of artistry possible.

AFTERWORD

These images are from a commercial that was produced by shooting the film in live action, tracing the figure and redrawing it by hand in the approved style, combining the live action and animation on an optical camera, and finally coloring all the drawings—frame by frame—using computer technology.

With technological advances, the world of animation is of course changing. Today, it is repeatedly suggested that the greatest development in animation is the computer-generated image. Indeed, so much is calimed for the once-humble computer that it may seem tempting for animators to put down their pencils and let the machines take over. Time and time again, we are told that the age of drawn animation is over, and that the age of the computer is upon us. The self-respect and confidence of animators appear to be at an all-time low, as they slink away from the fray, with huge silicon chips on their shoulders.

At the same time there is little doubt that the new computer-based technology can find a genuine place in the field of traditional animation, and animators ignore its potential at their peril. Without doubt, computer-generated images are superior in certain aspects of animation, and richly deserve the respect they are now given. Three-dimensional solid objects, for example, can be fairly easy (and often dramatically) turned and moved by the computer animator—sometimes, even more economically than by their traditional counterparts. Animated graphics, lettering, and symbols are other examples of the kind of images that can be better animated on the computer screen. In acknowledging our debt to the computer, however, let us not go too far and dismiss the real value of drawn animation.

Without the varied idiosyncrasies of a human personality, the computer is incapable of giving a living spirit to its creatios, and this is the secret ingredient of all great animation. As long as audiences continue to want subtle, sophisticated, and entertaining character animation—where we actually believe that the drawings we see are alive and real—then the role of drawn animation in filmmaking is assured.

This workbook is a confirmation of my belief that there is still life in the old tradition of drawn animation. The principles outlined are only the foundations of an apprenticeship, which takes a working lifetime to learn and perfect. No book, however complex or thorough, can ever teach all that there is to learn about any subject. Nevertheless, this workbook should provide the basic information for you to move forward on your own, to discover new and exciting landmarks. It is in your hands, and the hands of your successors, that the craft and tradition of drawn animation firmly rest, and I wish you well with this challenge.

INDEX

This is the first frame of an animation sequence. Flip the pages forward, to page 9, to see the sequence in animation.

CREDITS

Grateful acknowledgment is made to the agencies and clients for permission to reproduce artwork from the following animated films and commercials by Animus Productions Ltd.:

"Castella Cigars" sequences, produced for D'Arcy MacManus Masius (agency) and Imperial Tobacco Ltd. (client): pages 10–11, 24–25, 36–37, 118–119, jacket front cover (first row), jacket front flap (Watson-Guptill edition only).

Cathedral, produced for Unicorn Projects, Washington, D.C., made possible by financial support from the National Endowment for the Humanities (U.S.A.): pages 55 (bottom), 106–107 (bottom), 142–143, 154 (bottom left), 155 (bottom right and left), 156, 157 (top).

"Country Crunch," produced for J. Walter Thompson (agency) and Golden Wonder Crisps (client): pages 104–105.

"Cussons Classic," produced for Allen Brady and Marsh (agency) and Cussons (UK) Ltd. (client): page 152 (bottom).

Hokusai—An Animated Sketchbook, financed by the Arts Council of Great Britain: pages 26–29 (bottom), 46–47 (bottom), 80–81 (bottom), 90–91 (bottom), 124–127 (bottom), 136–137 (bottom).

"Hots Ribena," produced for D'Arcy MacManus Masius (agency) and Beecham Foods (client): pages 112–115 (bottom).

"KKB Three Bears," produced for Baums Mang Zimmerman (agency) and KKB Bank (client): pages 13, 14, 72–73, 160.

"Lamot Volcano," produced for Reeves Robertshaw Needham (agency) and Bass Plc. Lamot Pills Lager (client): pages 144–145 (bottom), 154–155 (top), 157 (bottom).

"Masterpiece Salad," produced for Landsdown Euro Advertising (agency) and TMF Foods (Smedley's) (client): page 146.

"Natural Crunch," produced for D'Arcy MacManus Masius (agency) and Aplen (client): page 140 (bottom).

"Potterton Boilers," produced for Apect Advertising (agency) and Potterton Boilers (client): pages 40–41 (bottom), 59, 60–61 (bottom), 71 (bottom), 108–109 (bottom), 129 (bottom), 130–131, jacket front cover (third row), jacket back flap (Watson-Guptill edition only).

"Ribena—Alien," produced for D'Arcy MacManus Masius (agency) and Beecham Foods (client): pages 38–39 (bottom), 82–83 (bottom), 153 (bottom).

"Sony Swan Lake," produced for Boase Massimi Pollitt (agency) and Sony (UK) Ltd. (client): pages 128 (middle), 154 (bottom right).

Supastars, copyright Tony White: pages 42–43 (bottom), 64–65, 74–75 (bottom), 86–87, 92 (bottom), 94–95 (bottom), 97–99 (bottom), 101–103 (bottom), jacket front cover (fourth row).

"Supersoft 'Once,'" produced for Boase Massimi Pollitt (agency) and Reckitt and Colman (client): page 158.

Untitled Leica reel, produced for Boase Massimi Pollitt: pages 1–8, 132 (bottom).

"Velvaglow," produced for Partnership in Advertising (agency) and Plascon Evans (client): pages 16–17, 44–45, jacket front cover (second row).

Grateful acknowledgment is also made to the design talents of Neil Ross, David Bergen, Tass Hesom, Bob McKnight, Gino D'Achille, and Dene Yegel.

The photographs on pages 120–121 and 125 are reproduced courtesy of Dover Publications, Inc., from Eadweard Muybridge, *Animals in Motion*, 1957.

Edited by Sue Heinemann
Designed by Bob Fillie
Graphic production by Kathy Rosenbloom
Text set in 12-point Sabon